© **Copyright 2024 - All rights reserved.**

You may not reproduce, duplicate or send the contents of this book without direct written permission from the author. You cannot hereby despite any circumstance blame the publisher or hold him or her to legal responsibility for any reparation, compensations, or monetary forfeiture owing to the information included herein, either in a direct or an indirect way.

Legal Notice: This book has copyright protection. You can use the book for personal purposes. You should not sell, use, alter, distribute, quote, take excerpts, or paraphrase in part or whole the material contained in this book without obtaining the permission of the author first.

Disclaimer Notice: You must take note that the information in this document is for casual reading and entertainment purposes only. We have made every attempt to provide accurate, up-to-date, and reliable information. We do not express or imply guarantees of any kind. The persons who read admit that the writer is not occupied in giving legal, financial, medical, or other advice. We put this book content by sourcing various places.

Please consult a licensed professional before you try any techniques shown in this book. By going through this document, the book lover comes to an agreement that under no situation is the author accountable for any forfeiture, direct or indirect, which they may incur because of the use of material contained in this document, including, but not limited to, α errors, omissions, or inaccuracies.

THIS BOOK BELONGS TO

Maze 1 - Medium

Maze 2 - Medium

Maze 3 - Medium

Maze 4 - Medium

Maze 5 - Simple

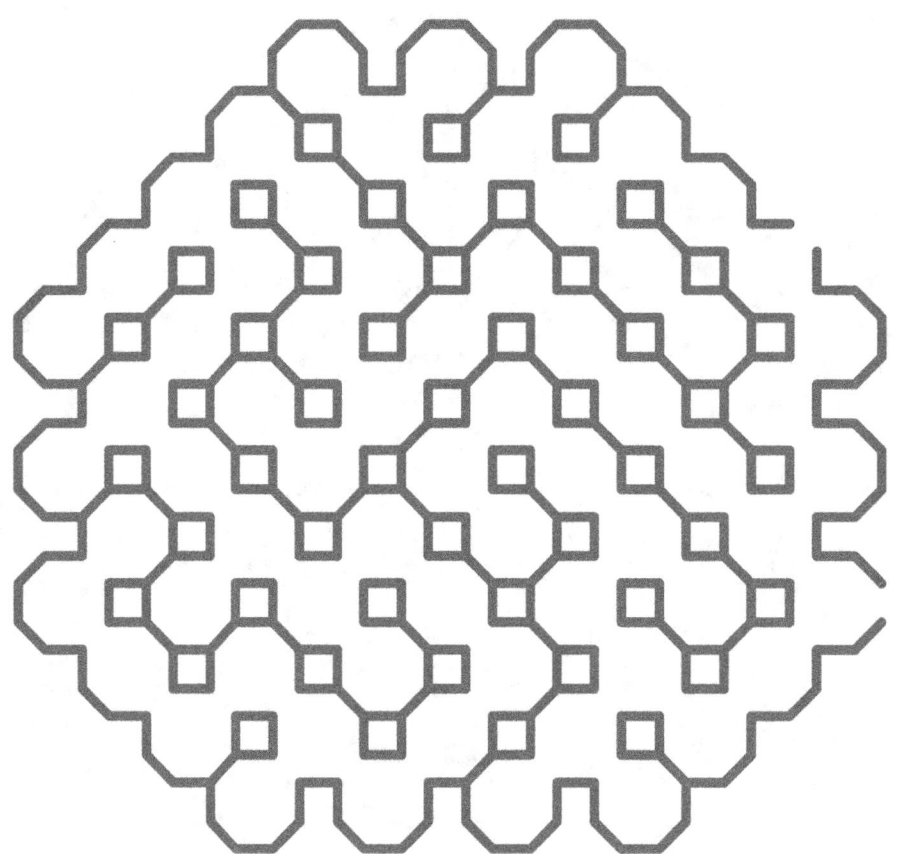

Maze 6 - Simple

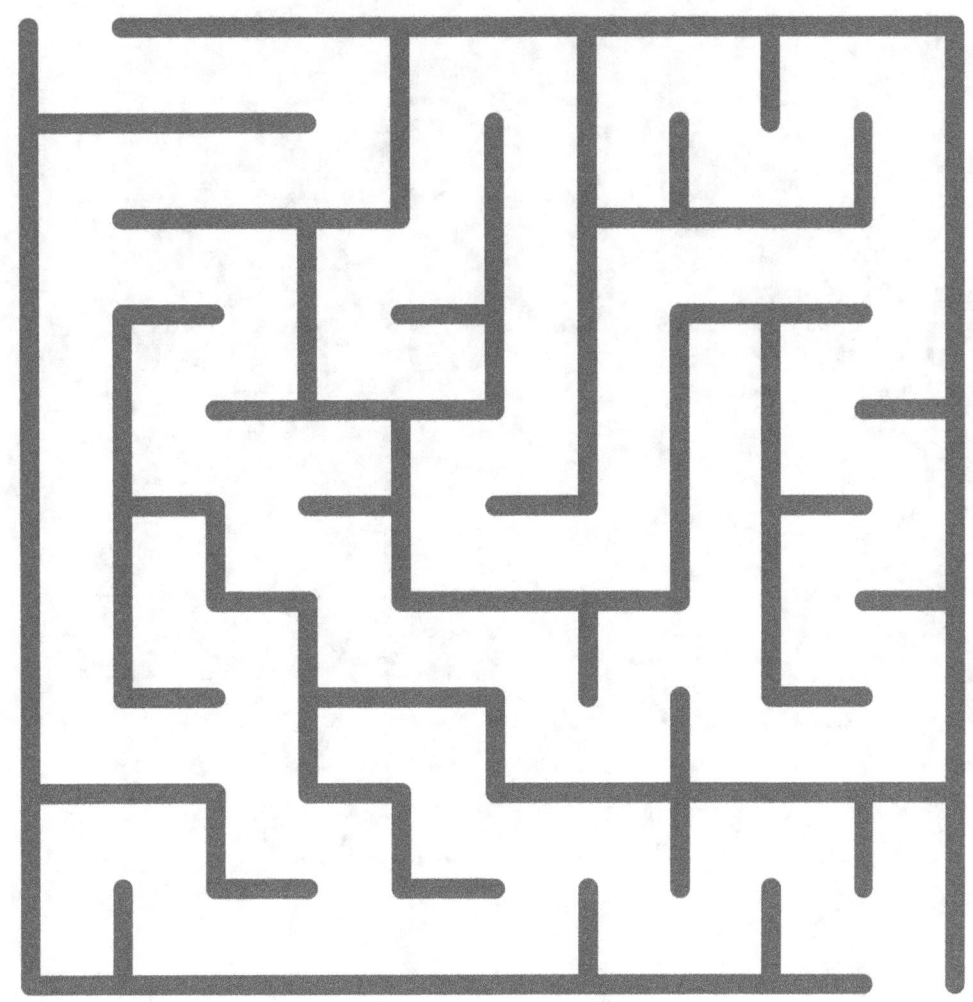

Maze 7 - Simple

Maze 8 - Medium

Maze 9 - Simple

Maze 10 - Medium

Maze 11 - Medium

Maze 12 - Medium

Maze 13 - Medium

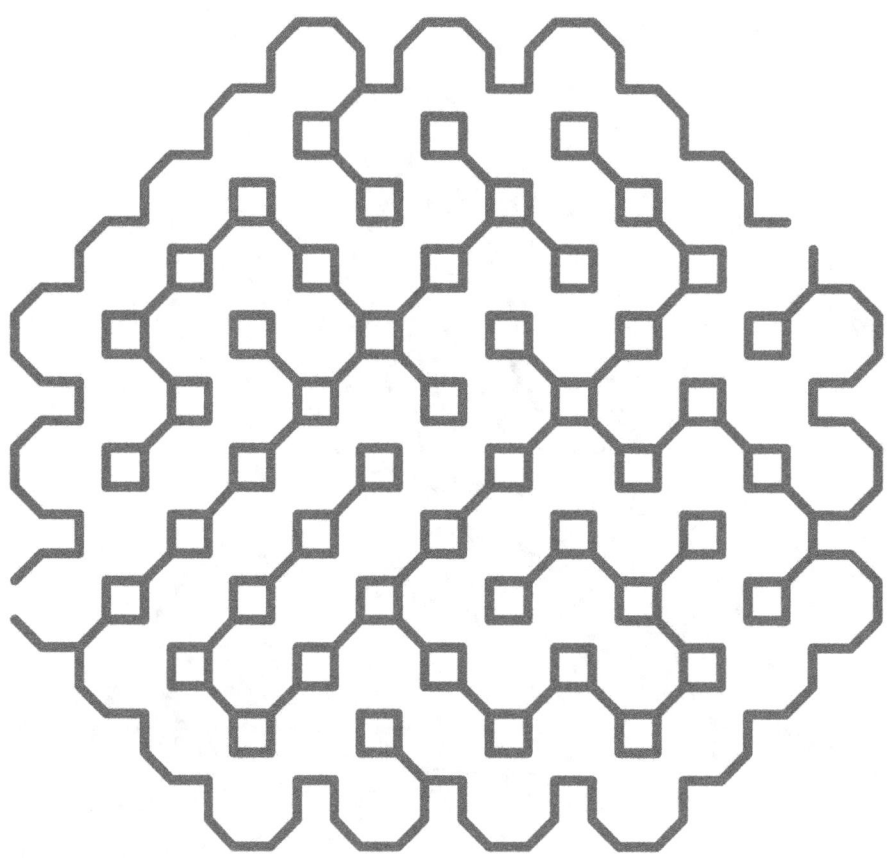

Maze 14 - Medium

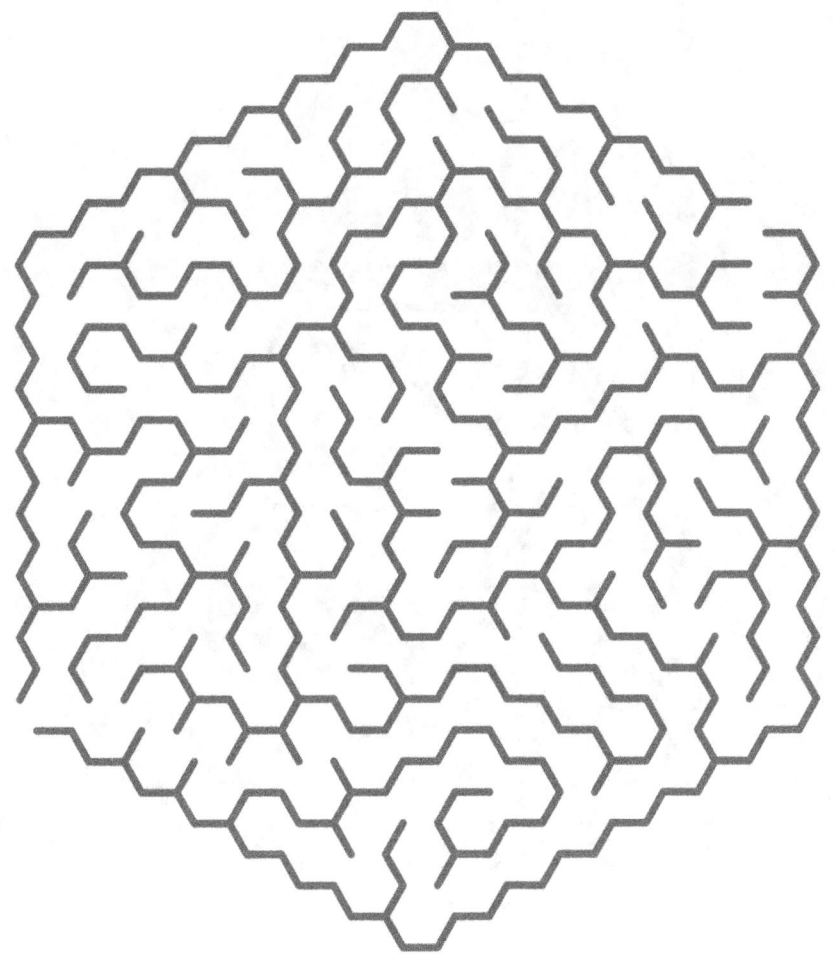

Maze 15 - Medium

Maze 16 - Simple

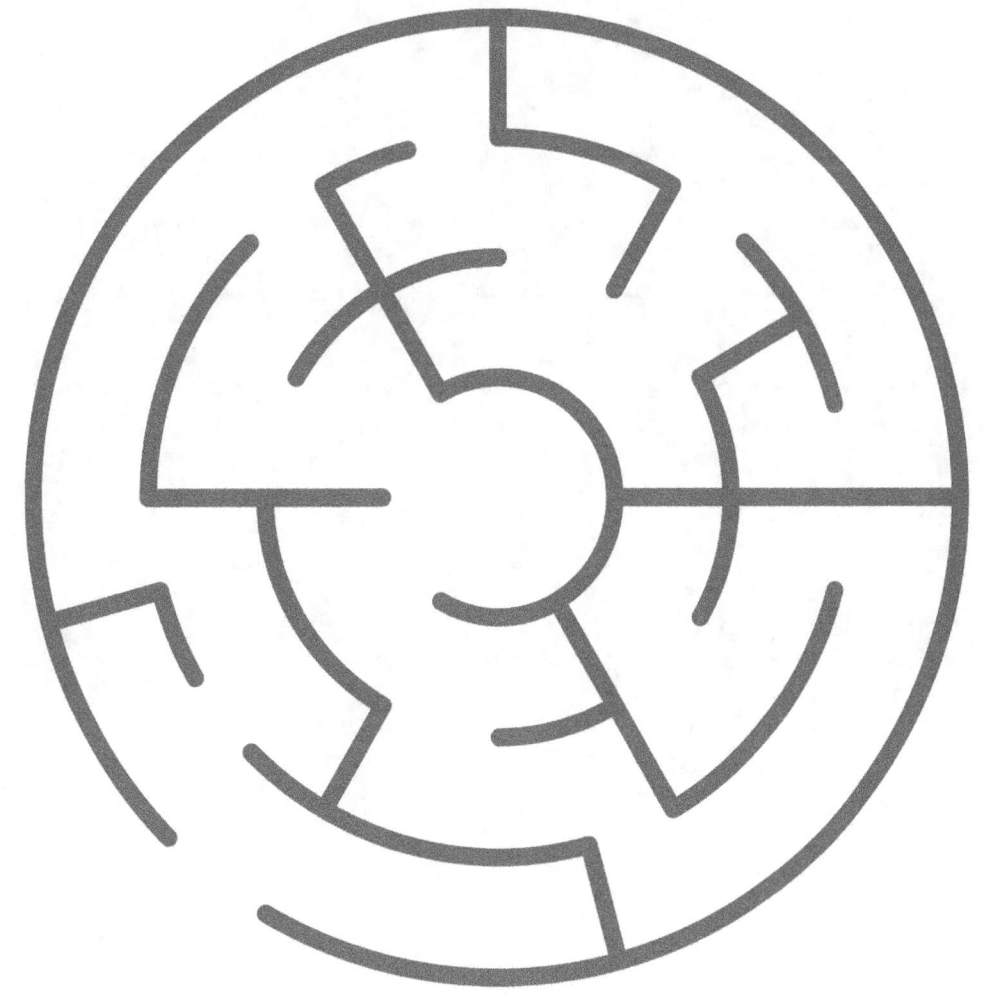

Maze 17 - Simple

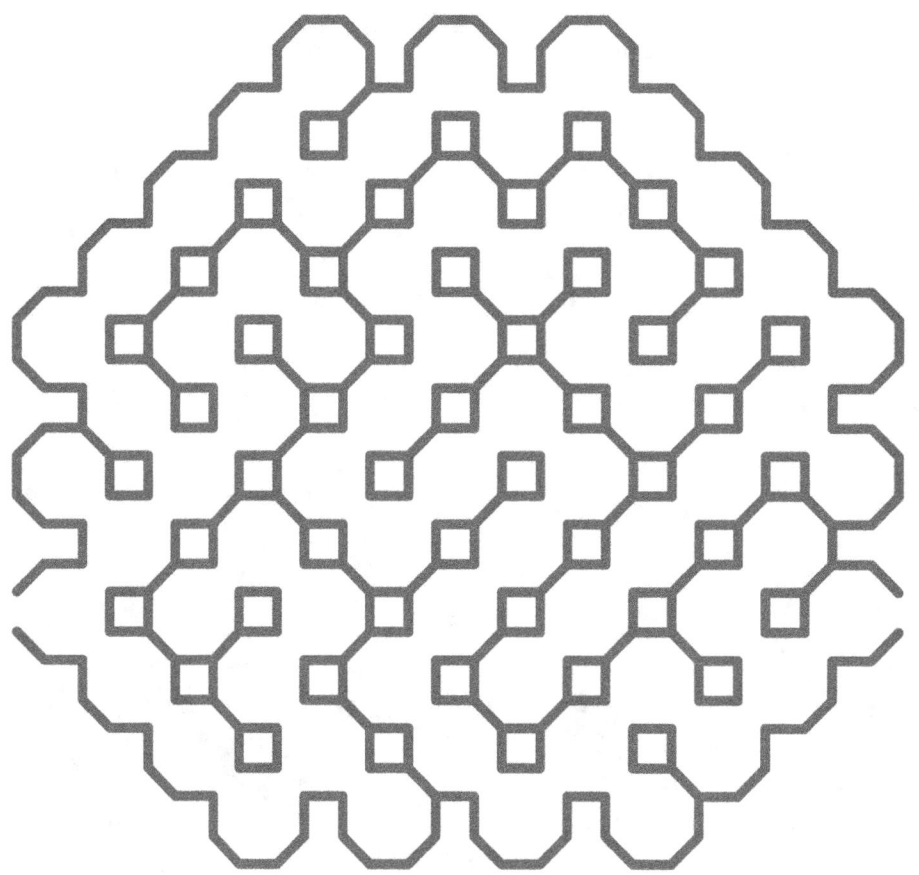

Maze 18 - Medium

Maze 19 - Medium

Maze 20 - Simple

Maze 22 - Simple

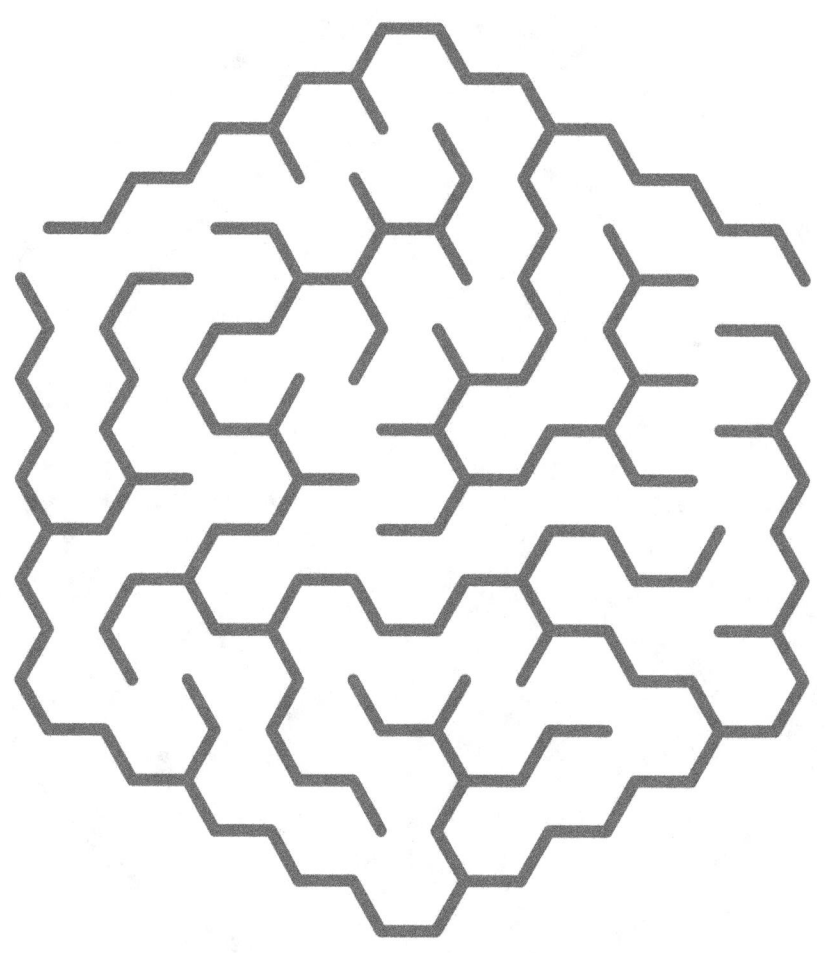

Maze 21 - Simple

Maze 22 - Simple

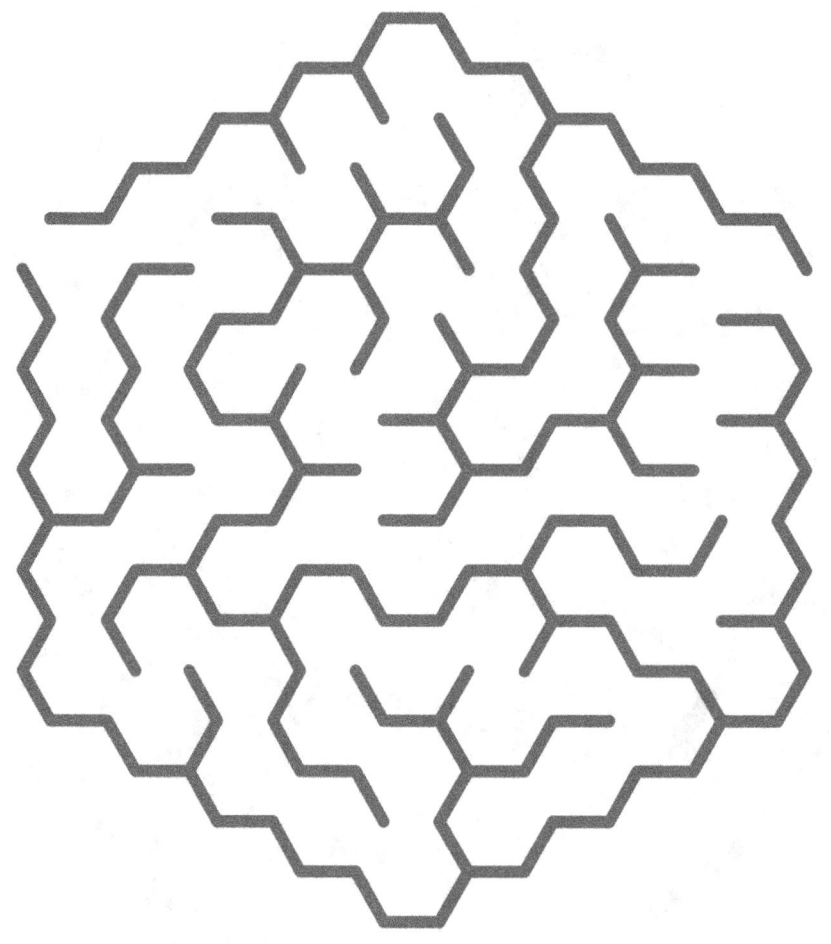

Maze 23 - Medium

Maze 24 - Simple

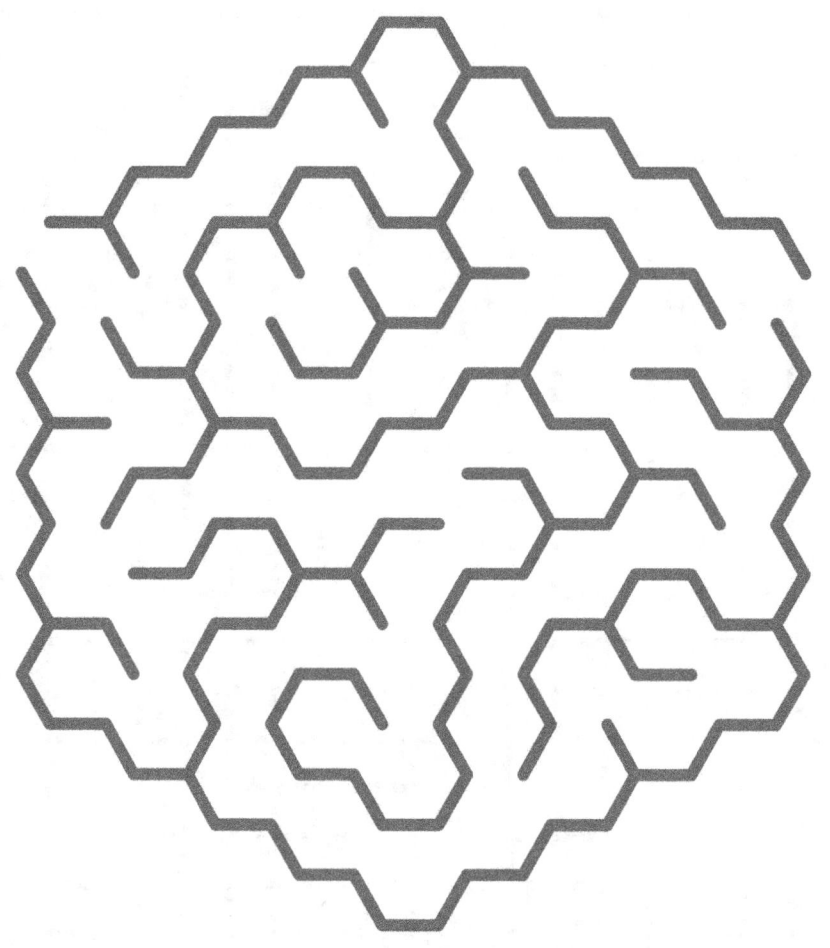

Maze 25 - Simple

Maze 26 - Medium

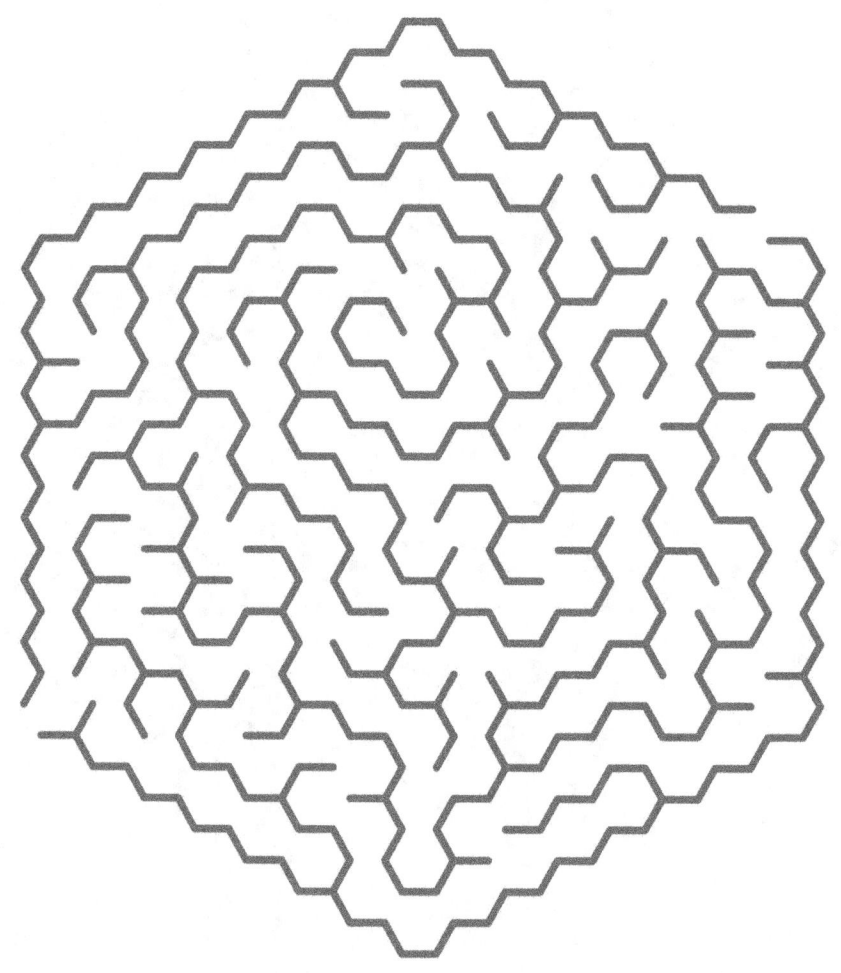

Maze 27 - Simple

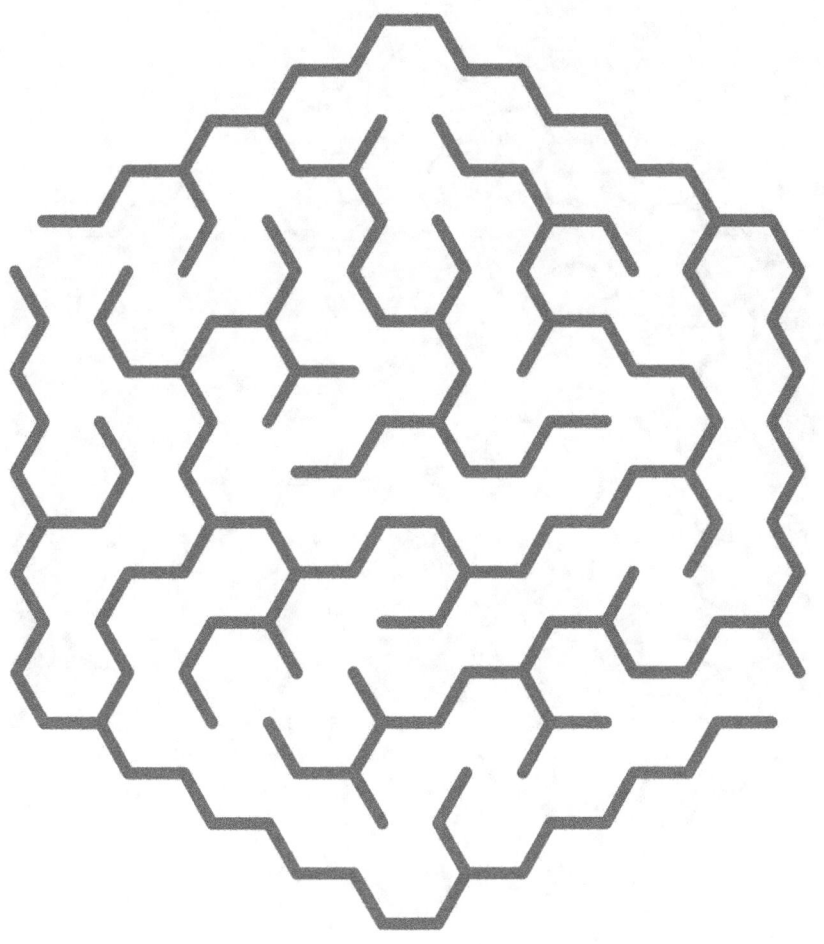

Maze 28 - Medium

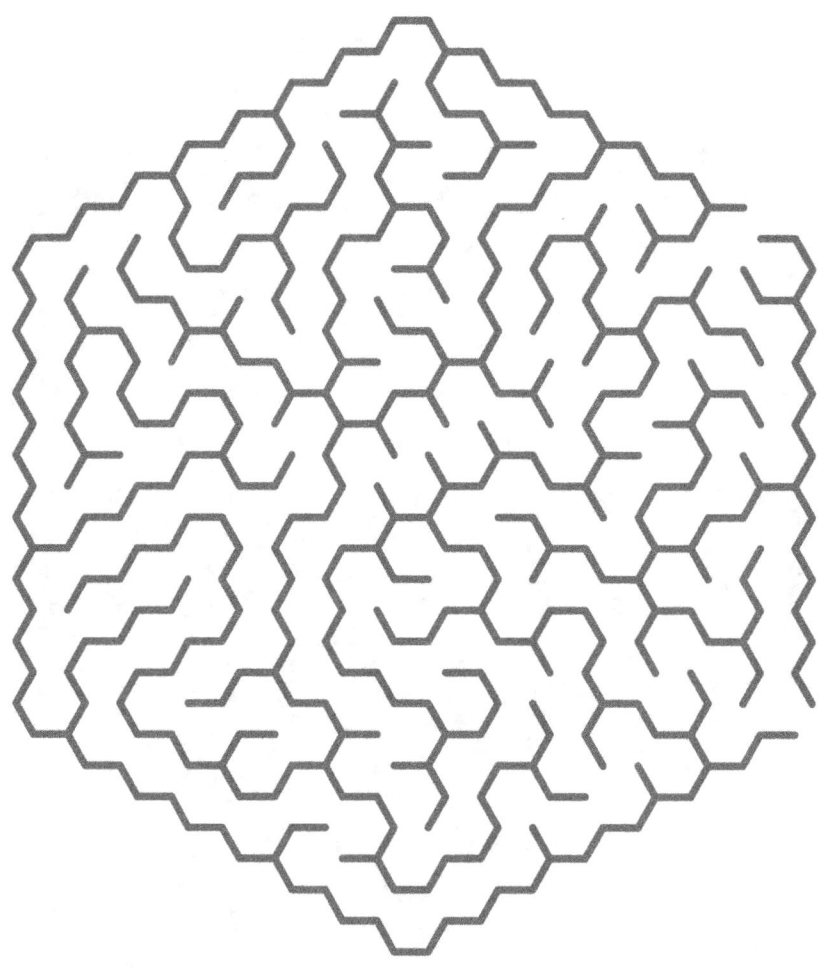

Maze 29 - Medium

Maze 30 - Medium

Maze 31 - Simple

Maze 32 - Medium

Maze 33 - Simple

Maze 34 - Medium

Maze 35 - Simple

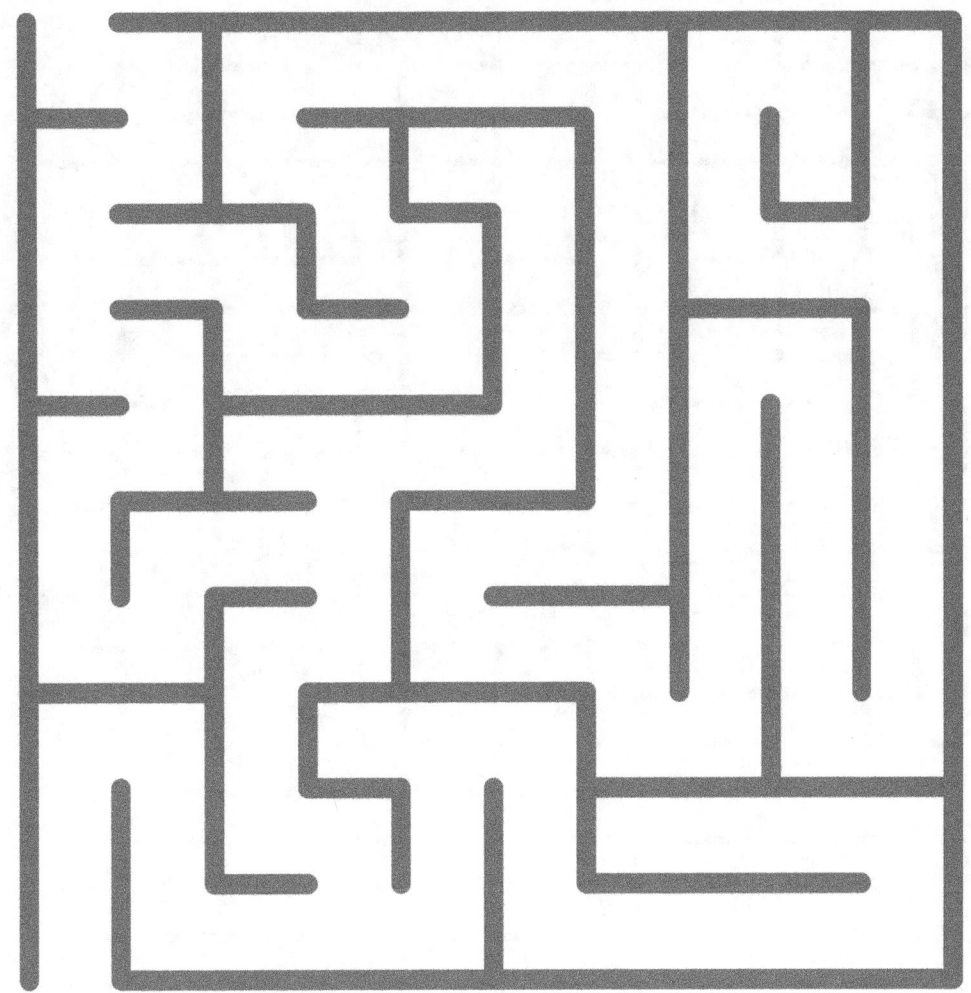

Maze 36 - Medium

Maze 37 - Medium

Maze 38 - Medium

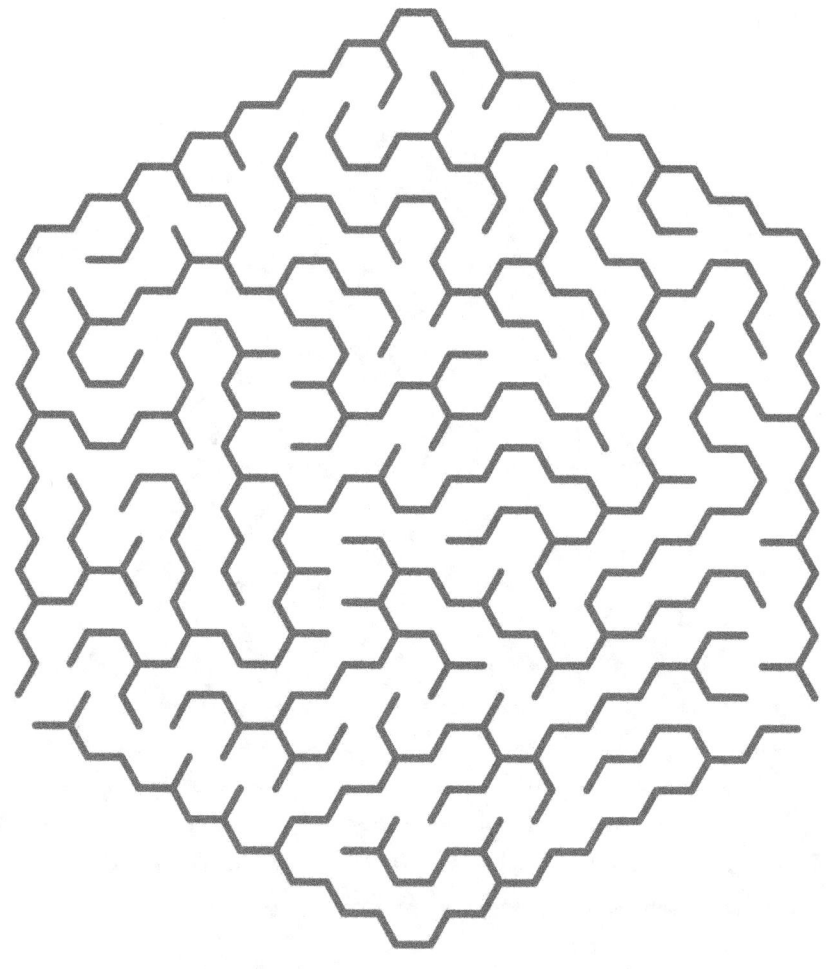

Maze 39 - Medium

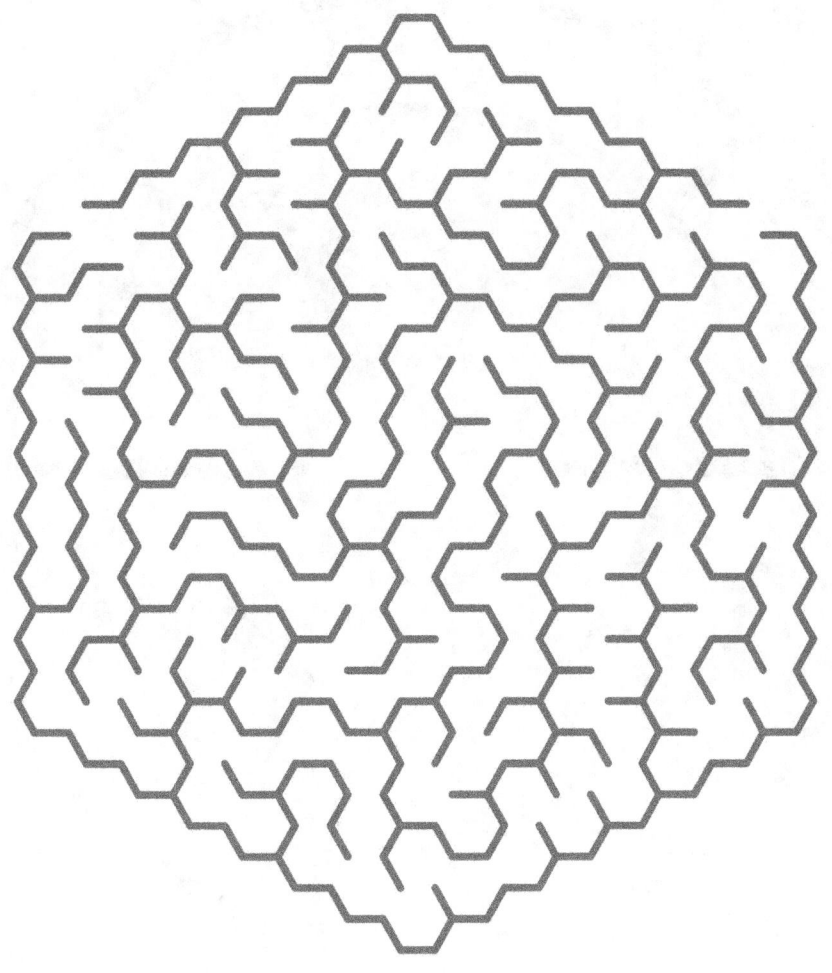

Maze 40 - Simple

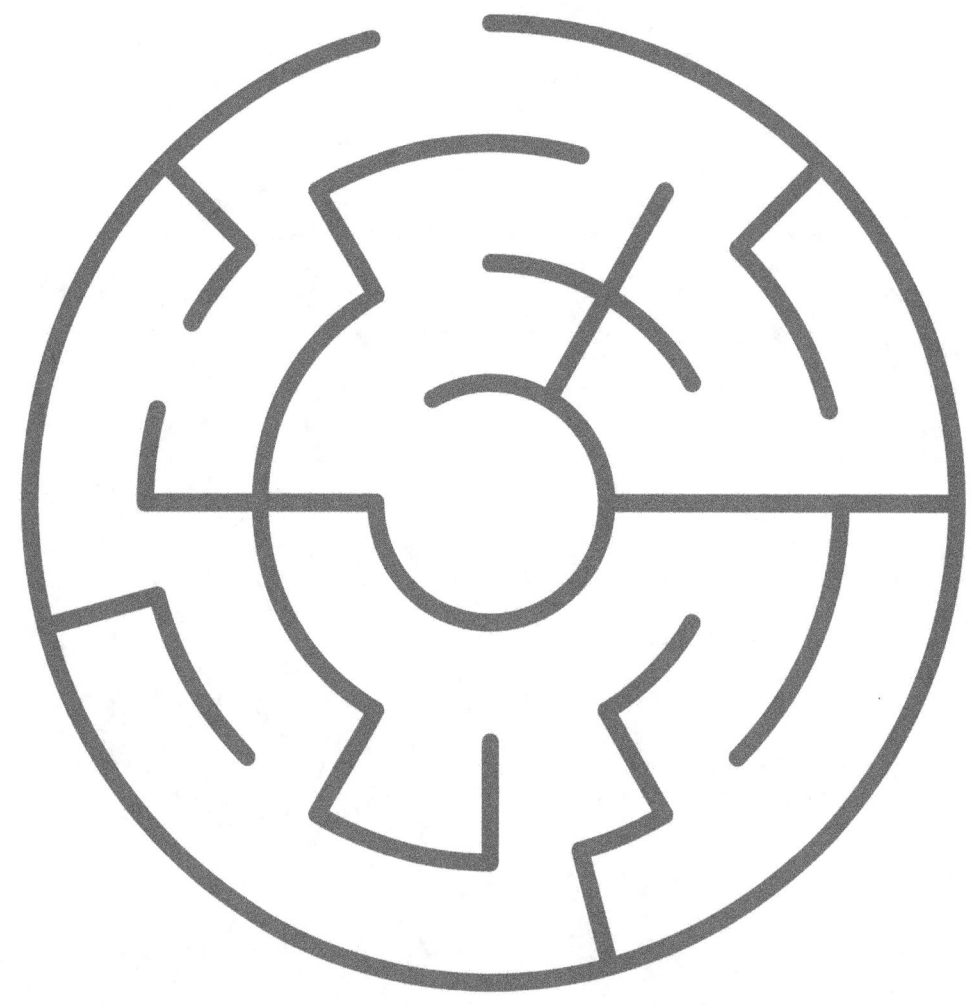

Maze 41 - Simple

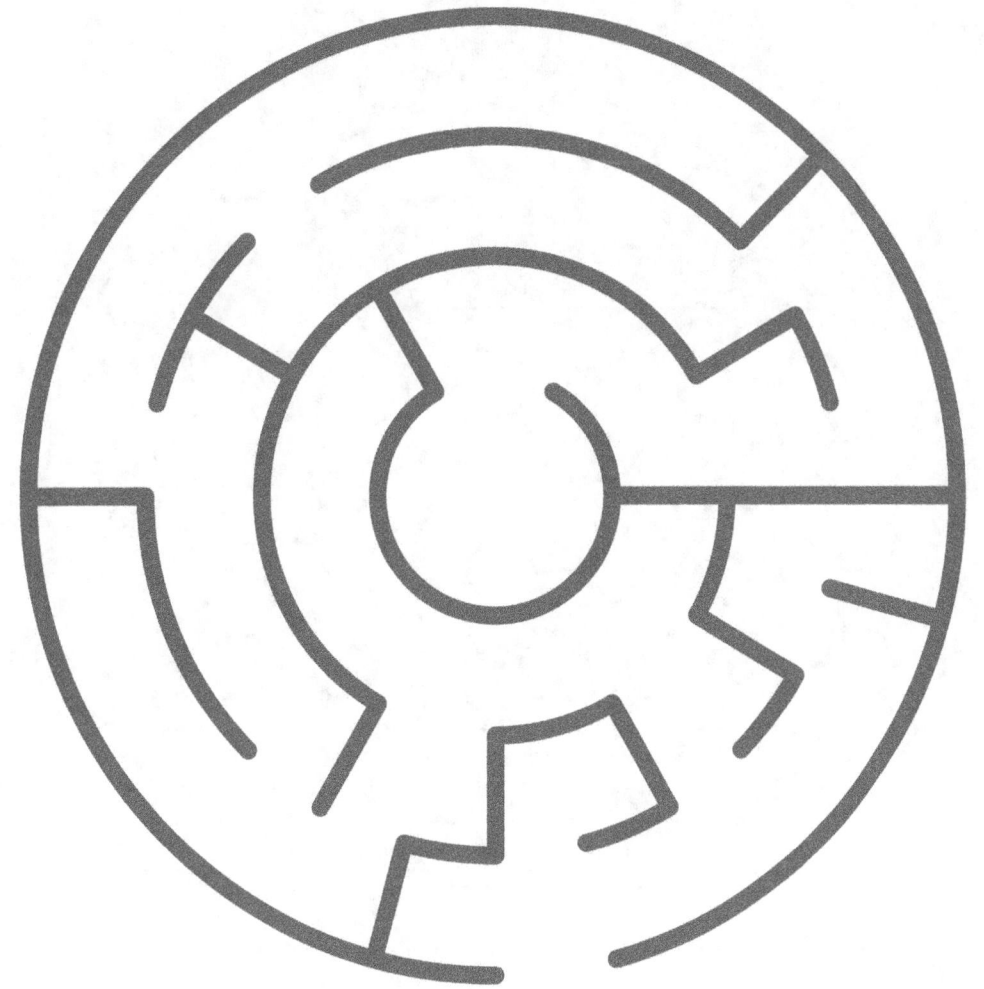

Maze 42 - Medium

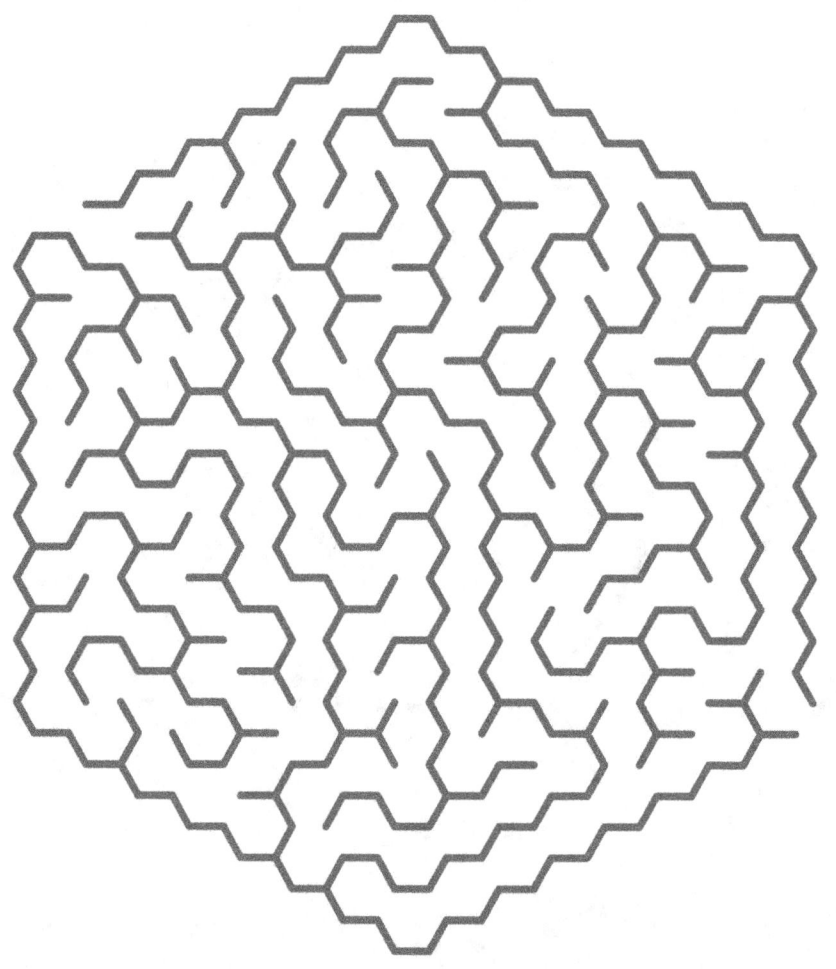

Maze 43 - Medium

Maze 44 - Simple

Maze 45 - Medium

Maze 46 - Simple

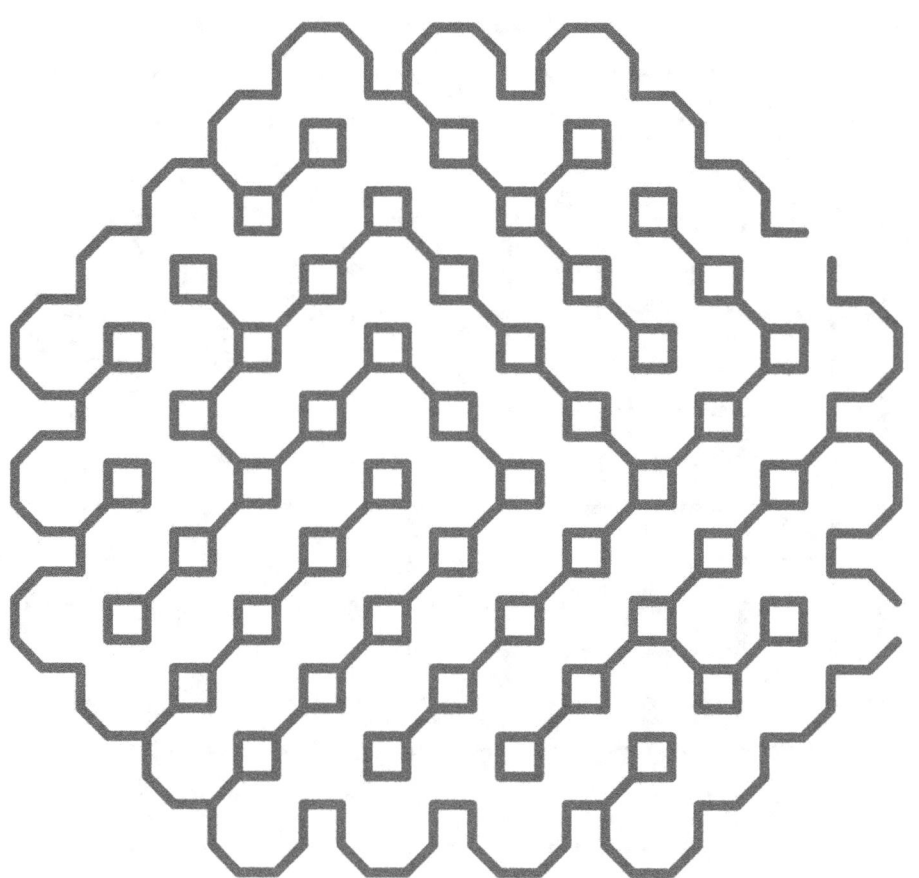

Maze 47 - Simple

Maze 48 - Simple

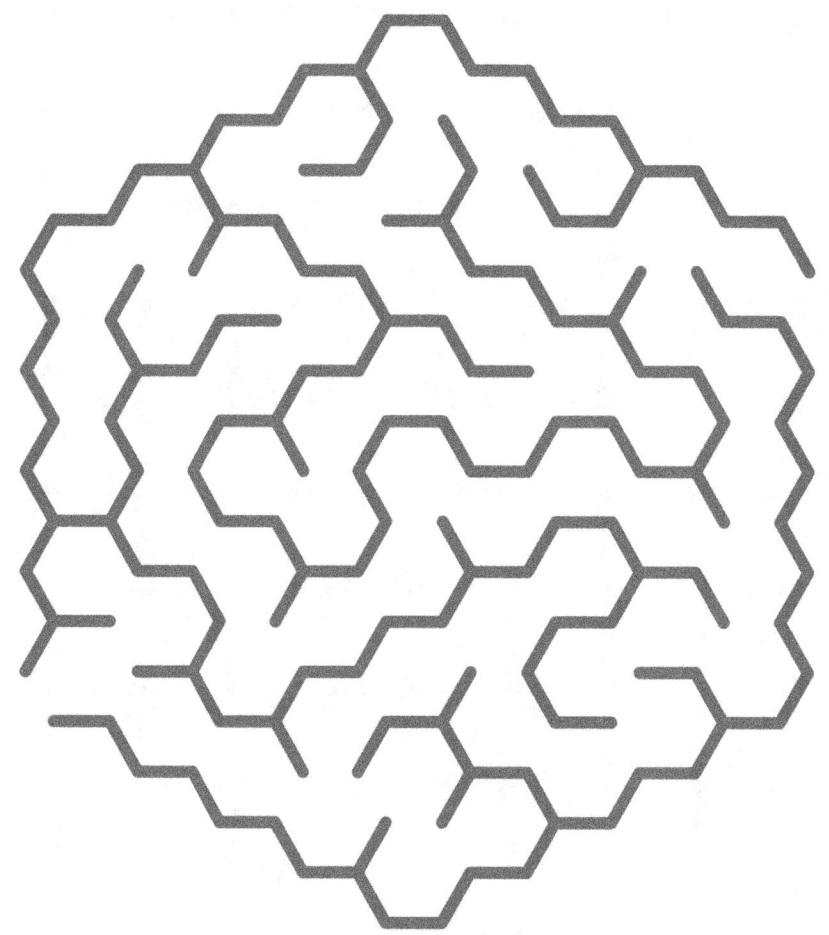

Maze 49 - Simple

Maze 50 - Medium

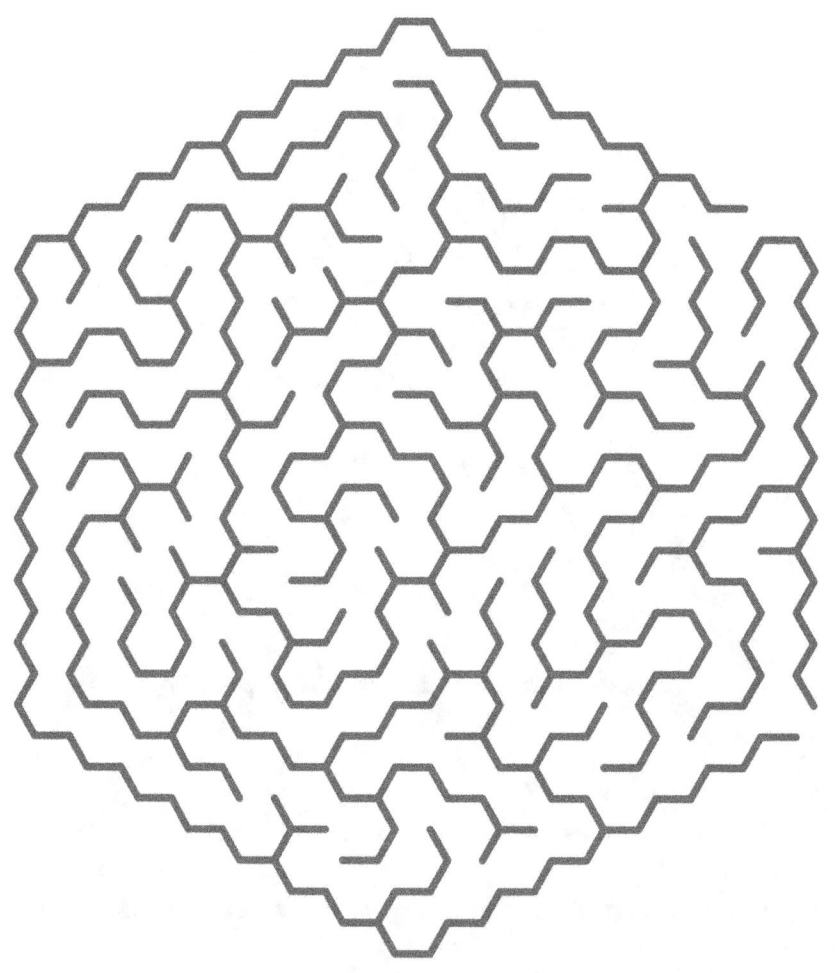

Maze 51 - Simple

Maze 52 - Medium

Maze 53 - Medium

Maze 54 - Medium

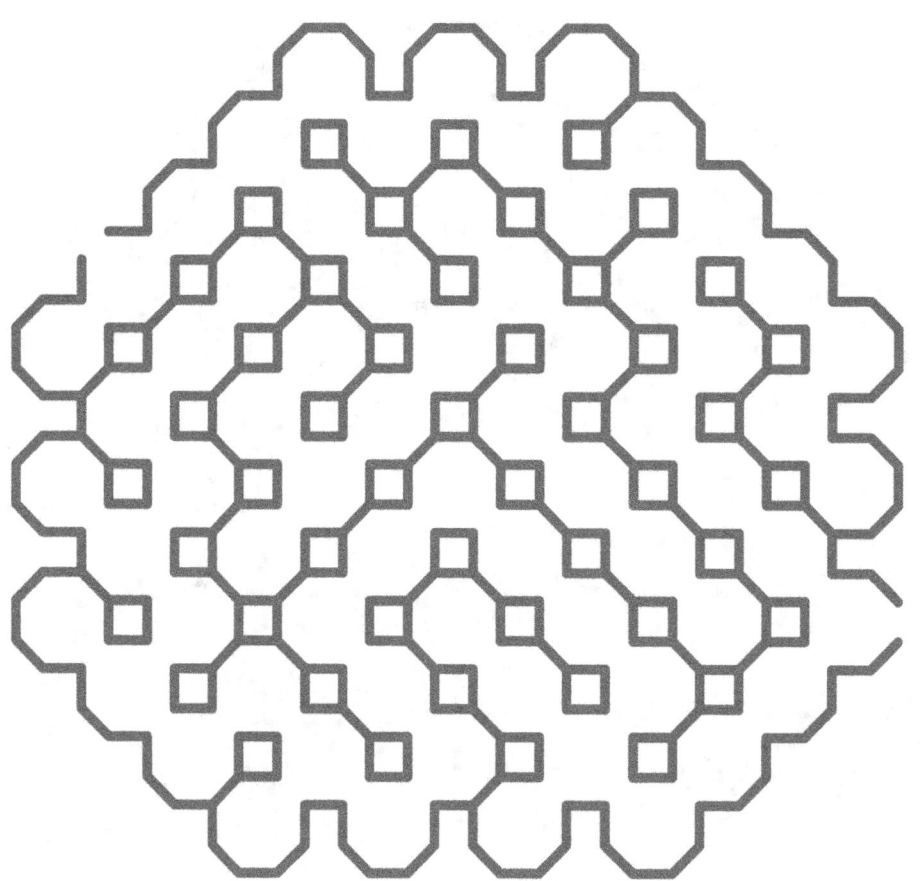

Maze 55 - Simple

Maze 56 - Medium

Maze 57 - Simple

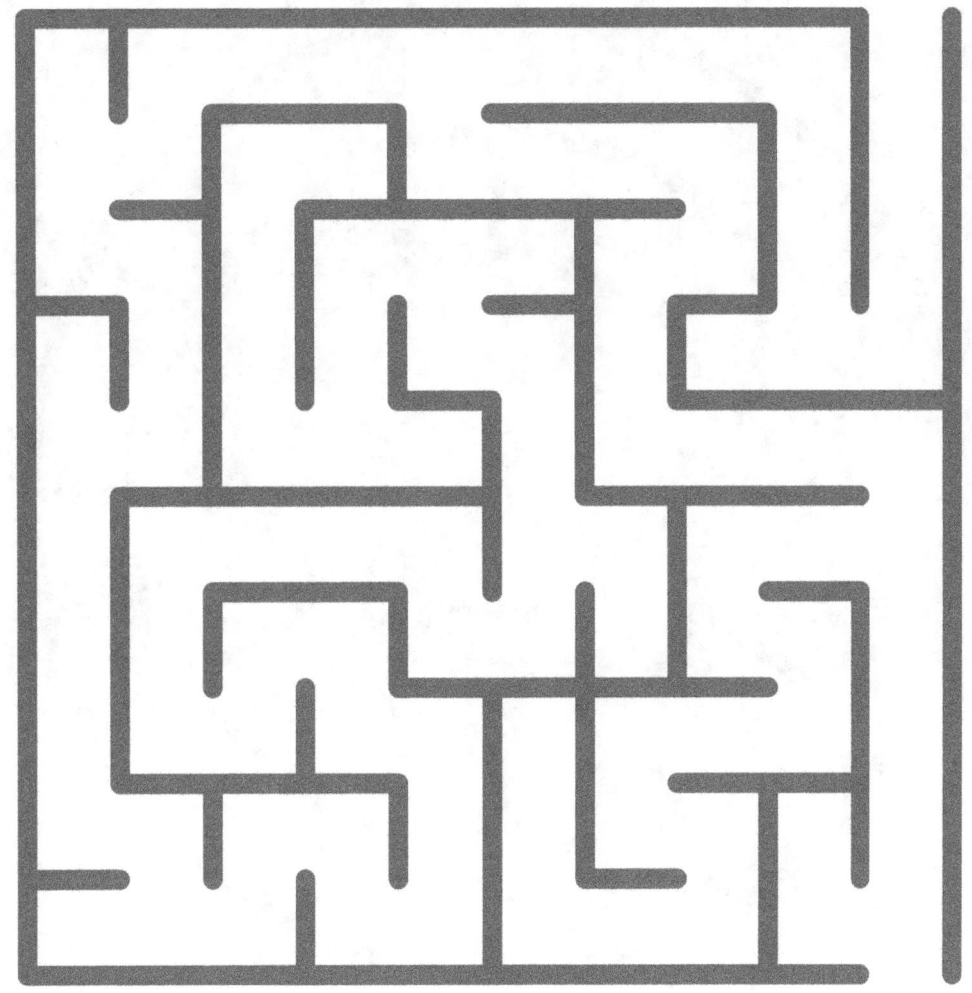

Maze 58 - Simple

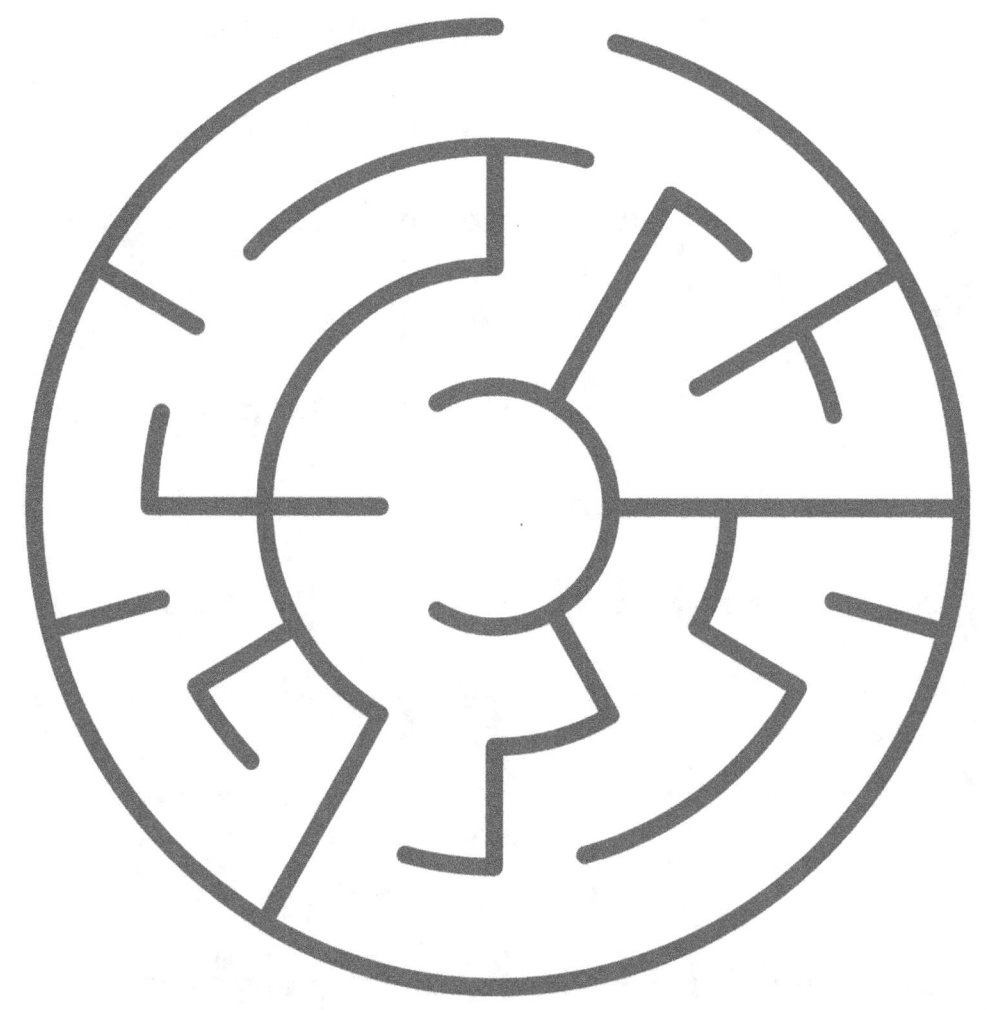

Maze 59 - Medium

Maze 60 - Medium

Maze 61 - Medium

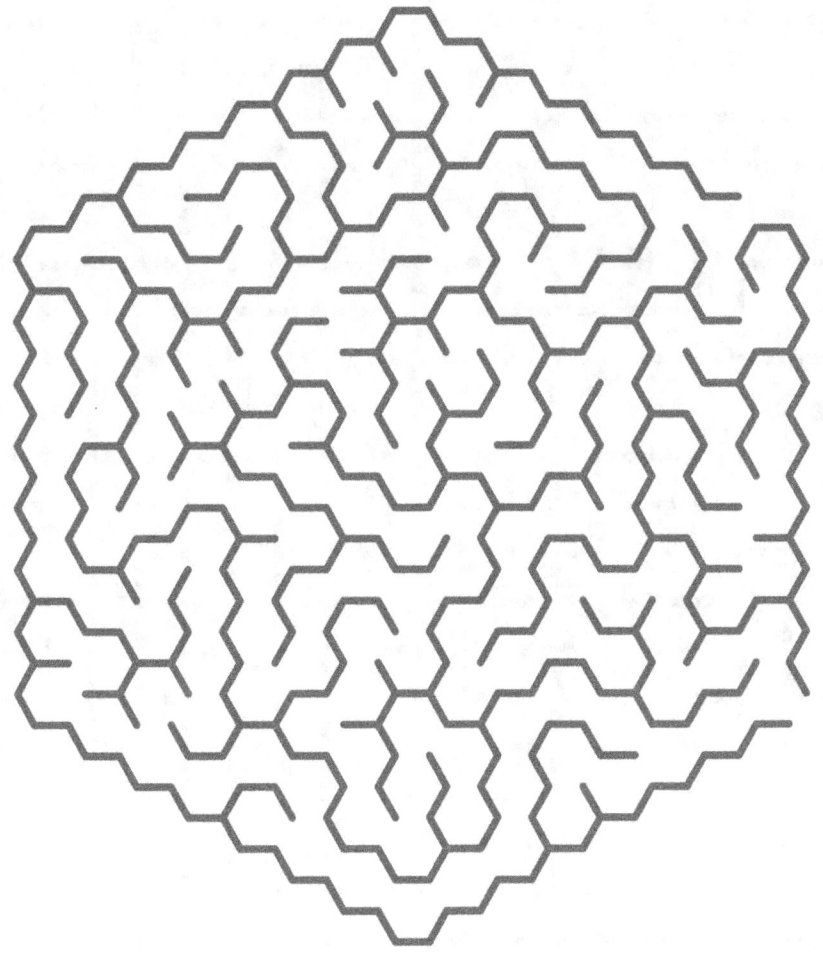

Maze 62 - Medium

Maze 63 - Simple

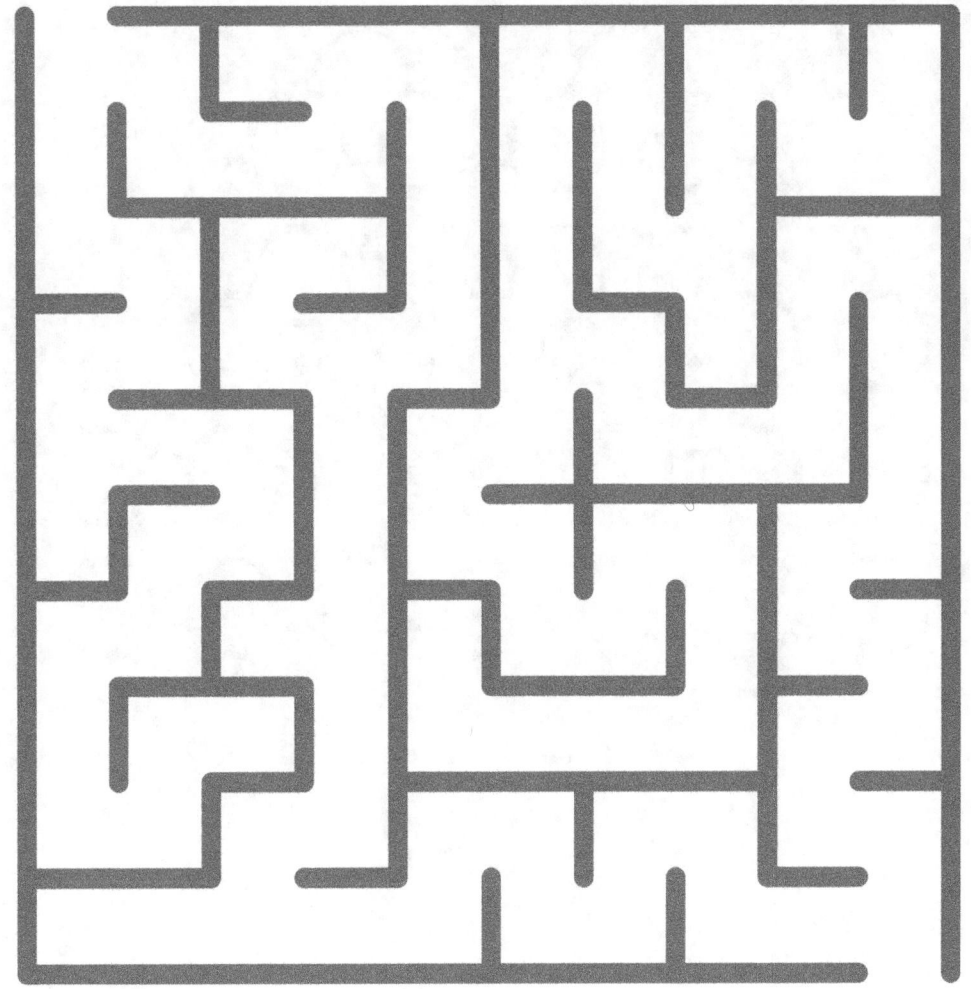

Maze 64 - Medium

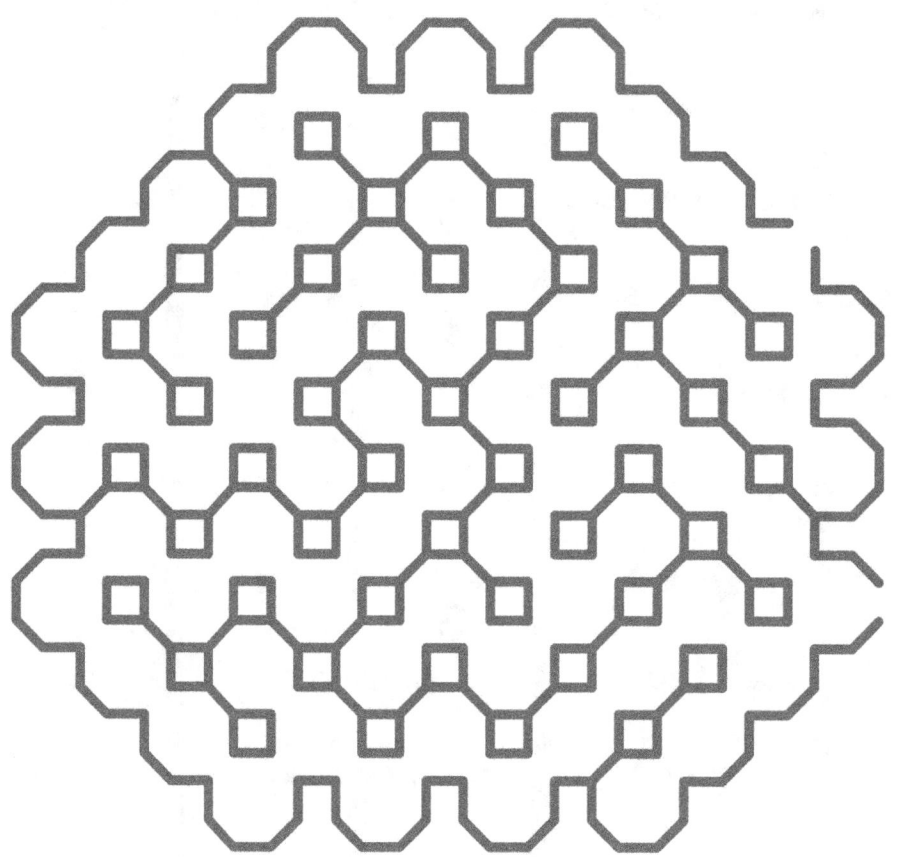

Maze 65 - Simple

Maze 66 - Medium

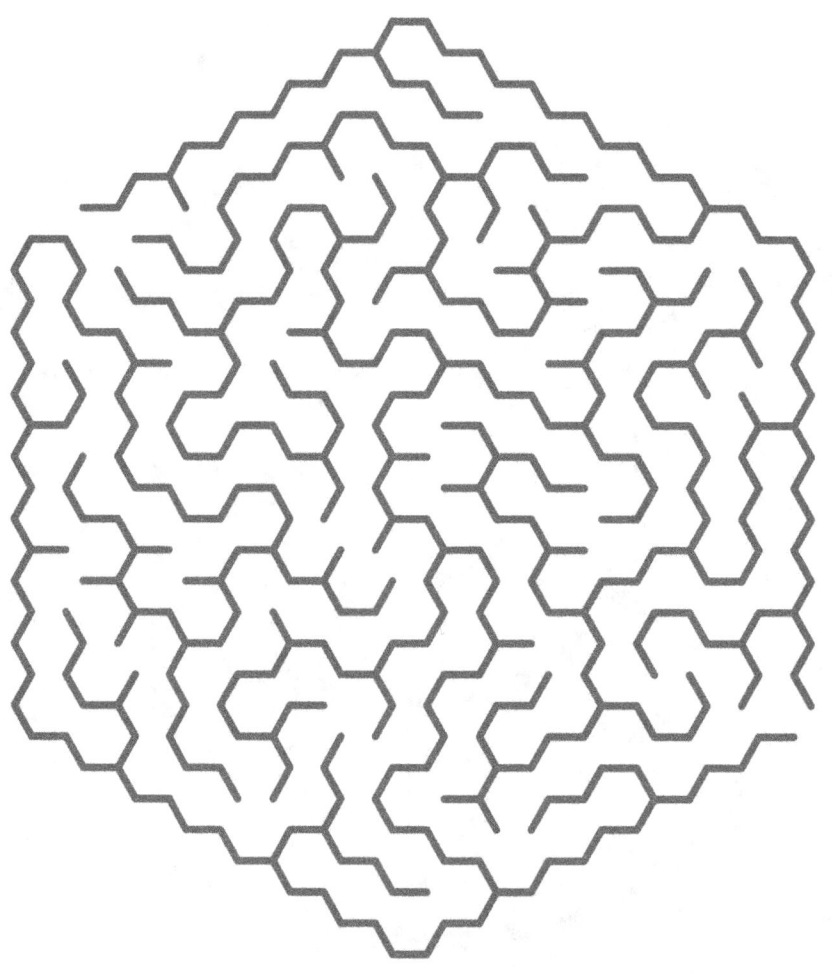

Maze 67 - Simple

Maze 68 - Simple

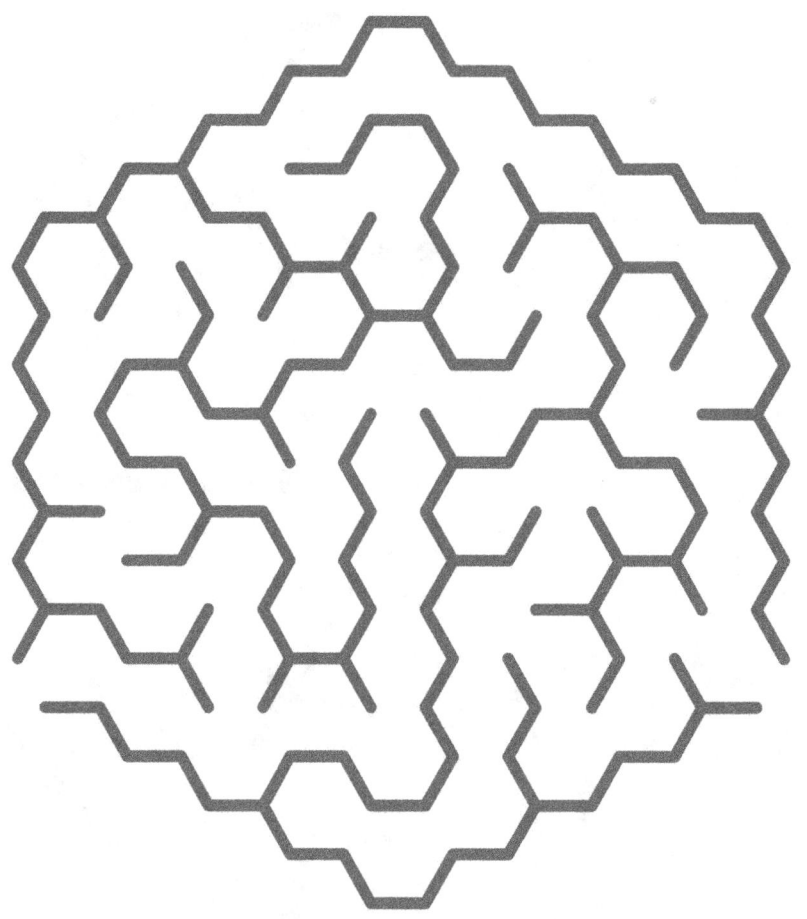

Maze 69 - Medium

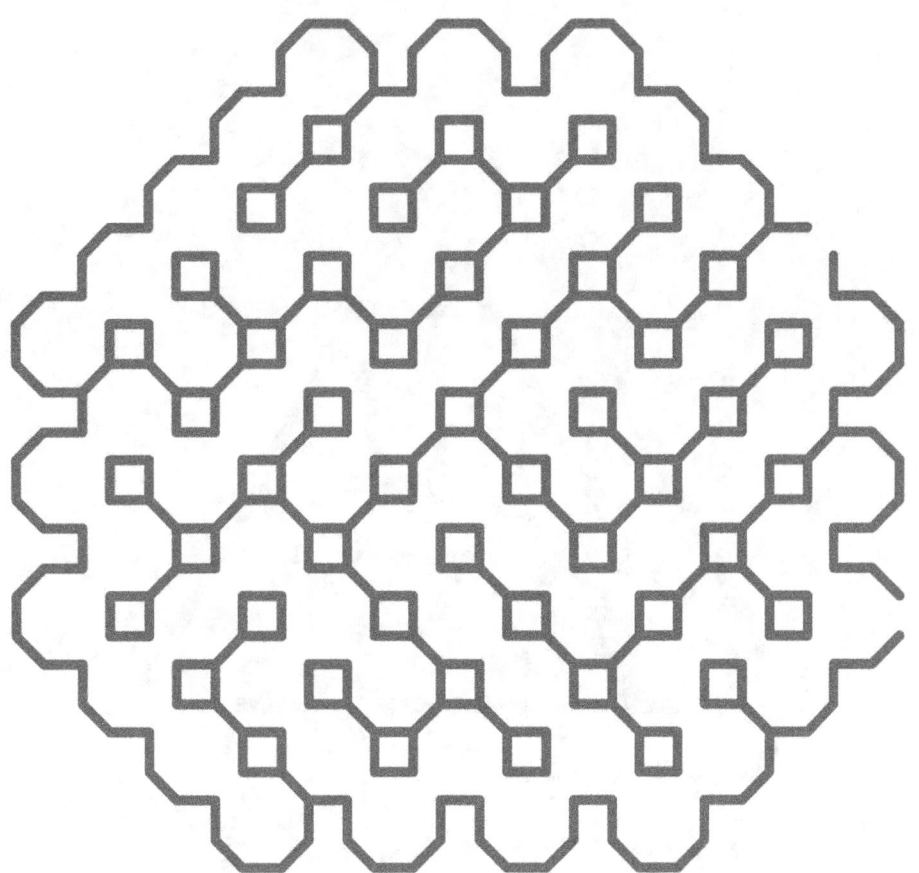

Maze 70 - Simple

Maze 71 - Medium

Maze 72 - Medium

Maze 73 - Medium

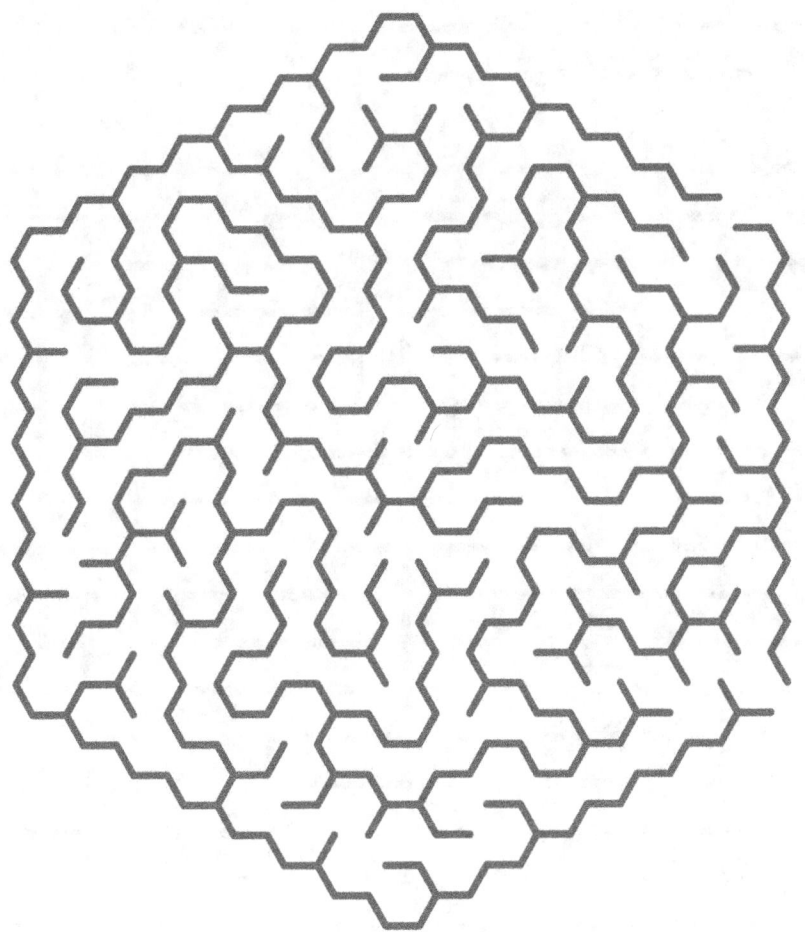

Maze 74 - Medium

Maze 75 - Medium

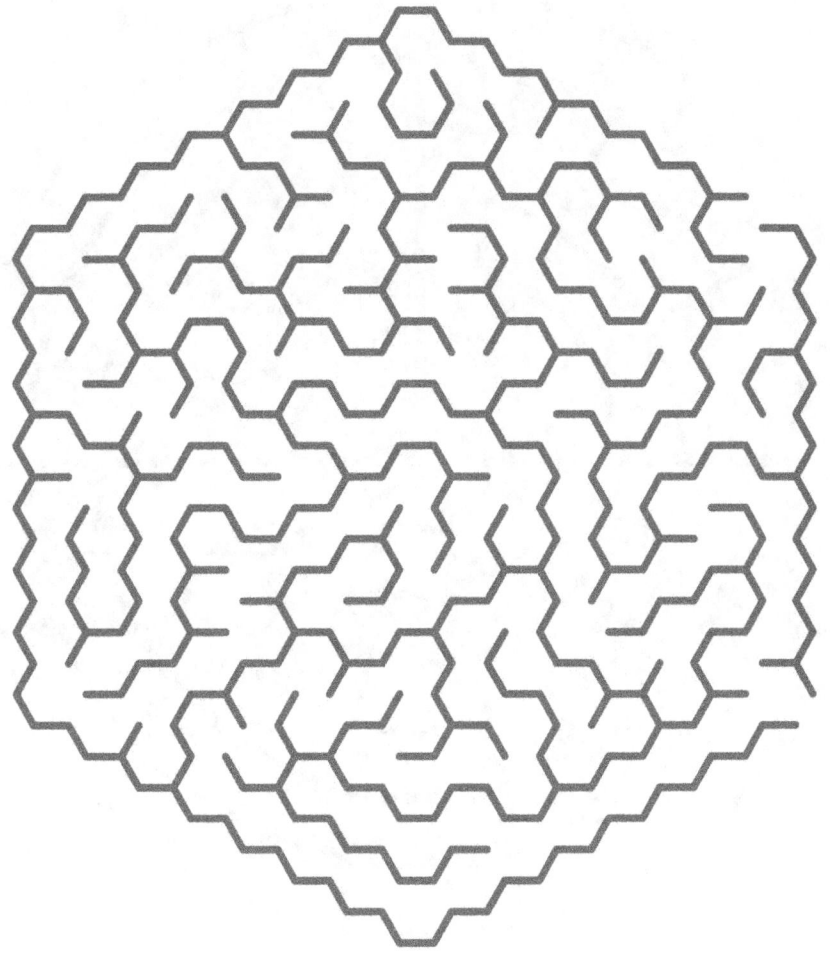

Maze 76 - Medium

Maze 77 - Medium

Maze 78 - Simple

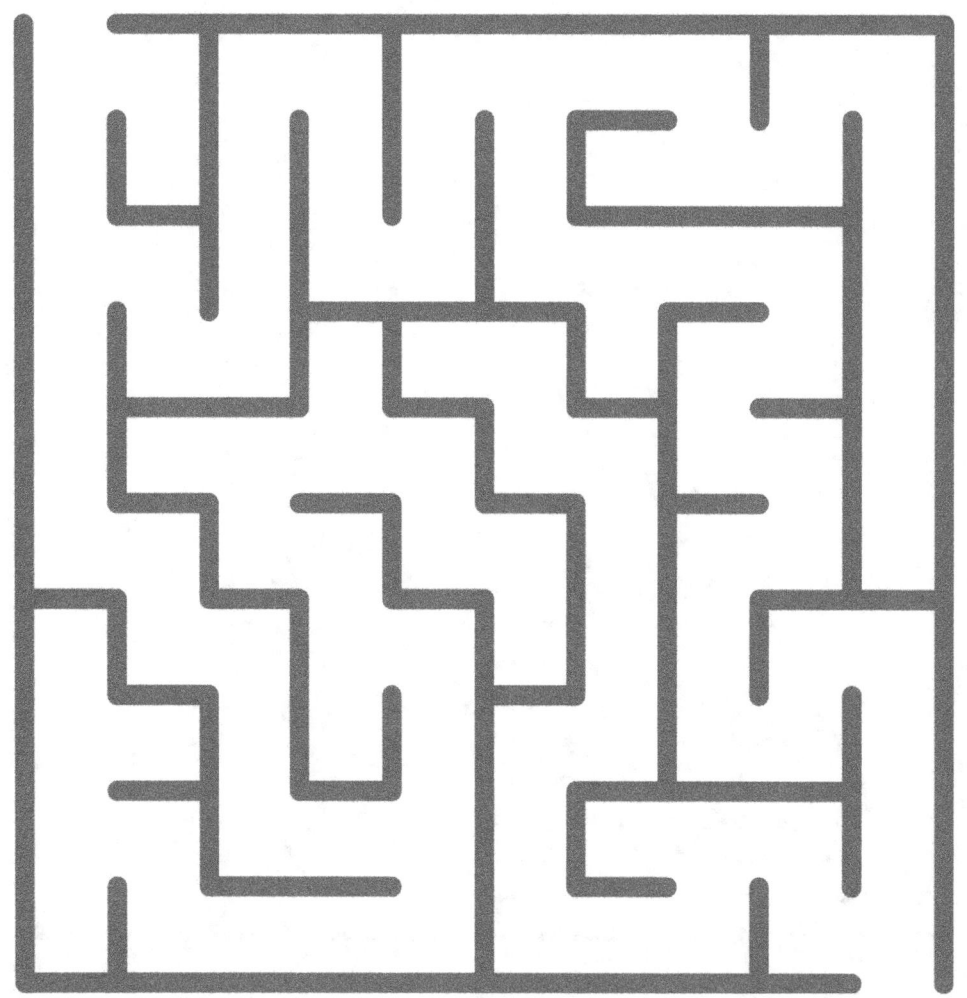

Maze 79 - Simple

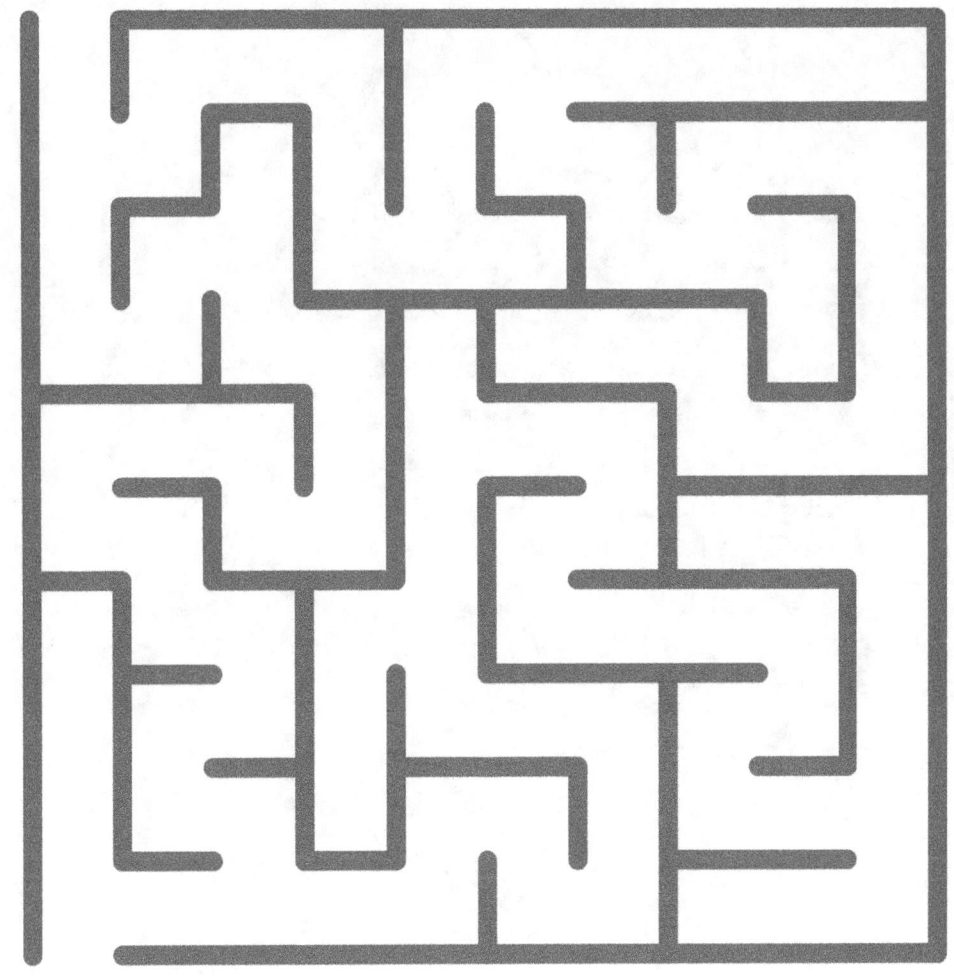

Maze 80 - Simple

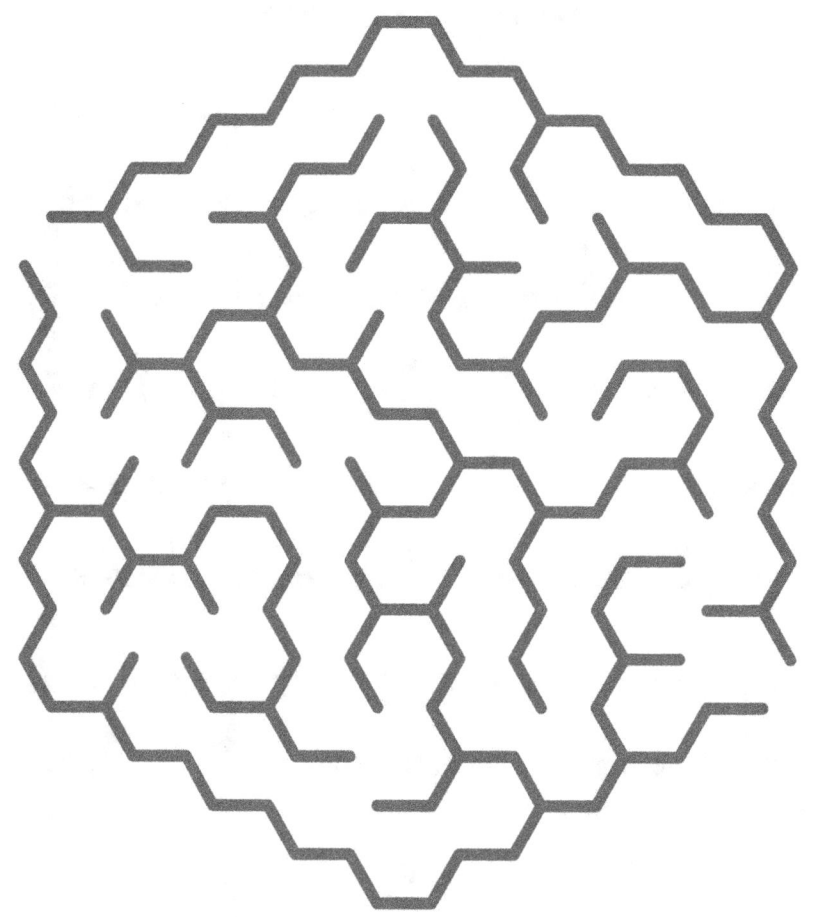

Maze 81 - Medium

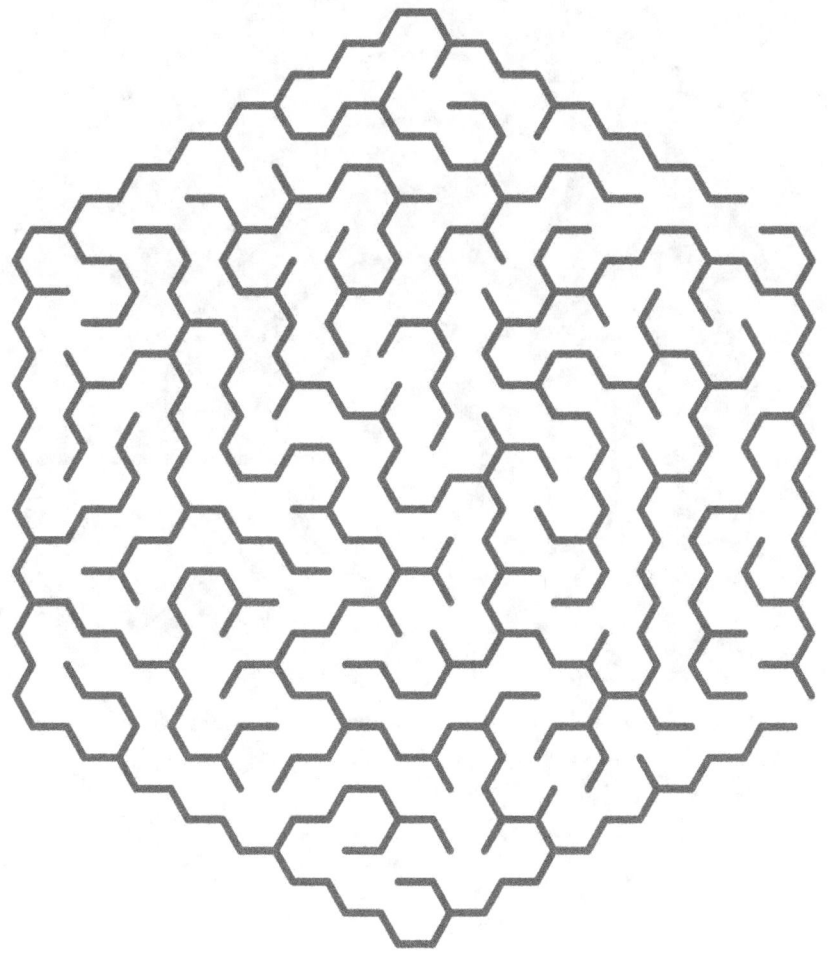

Maze 82 - Medium

Maze 83 - Simple

Maze 84 - Simple

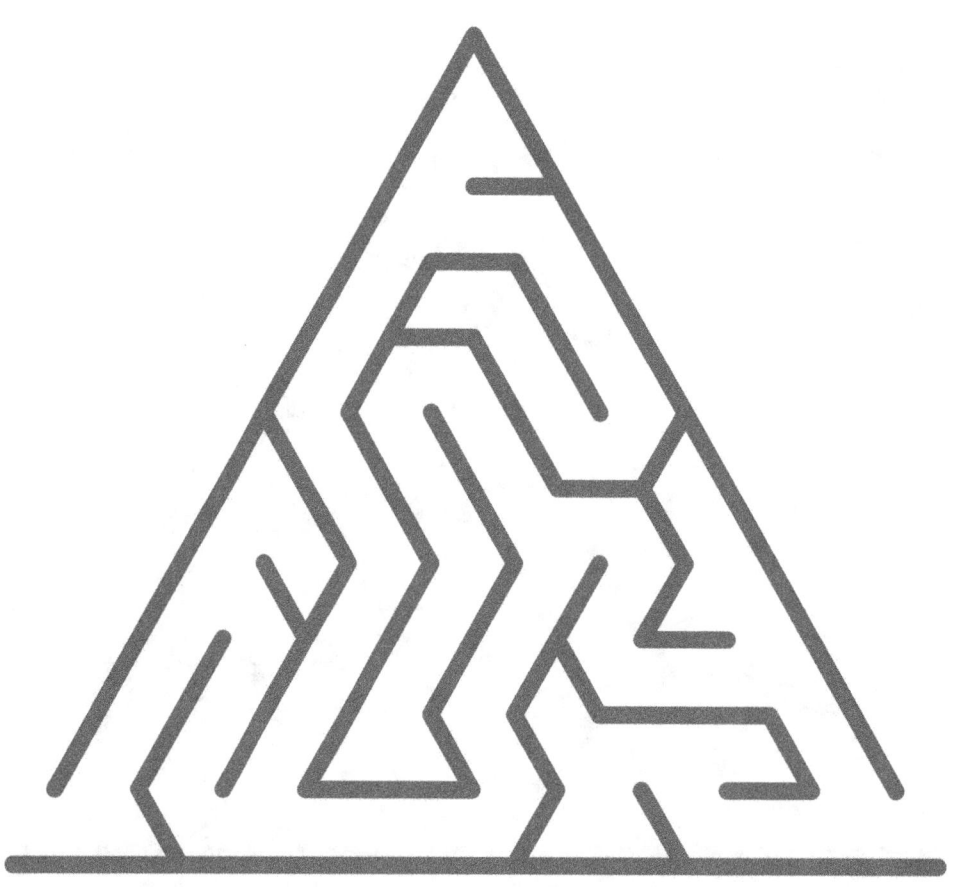

Maze 85 - Medium

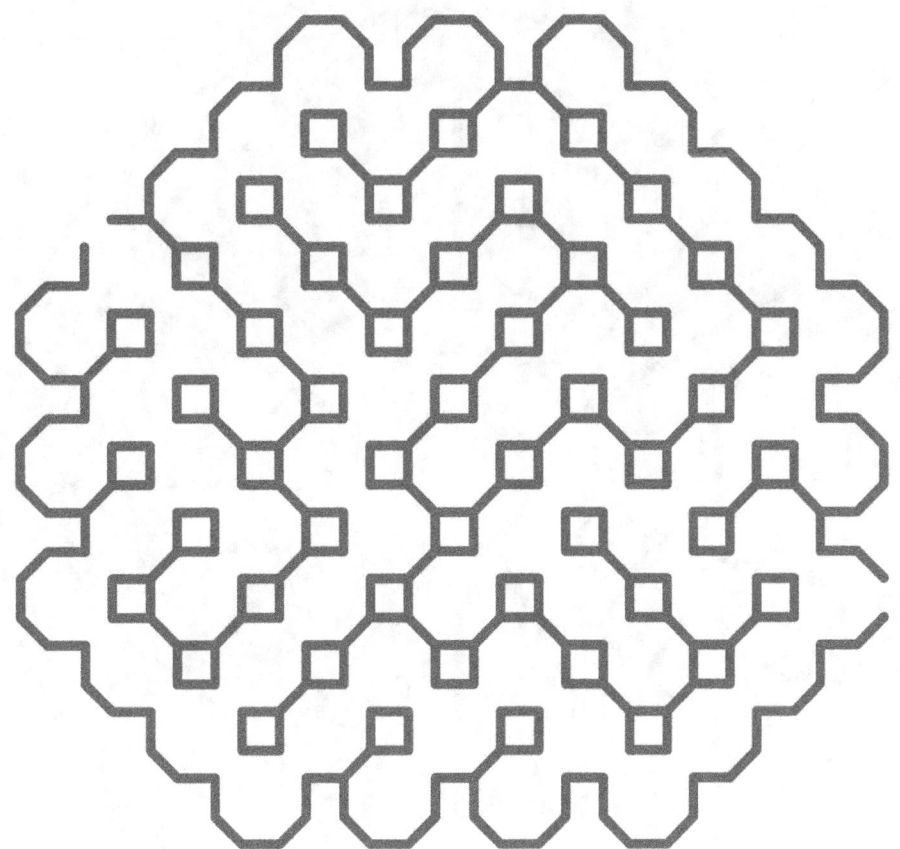

Maze 86 - Medium

Maze 87 - Simple

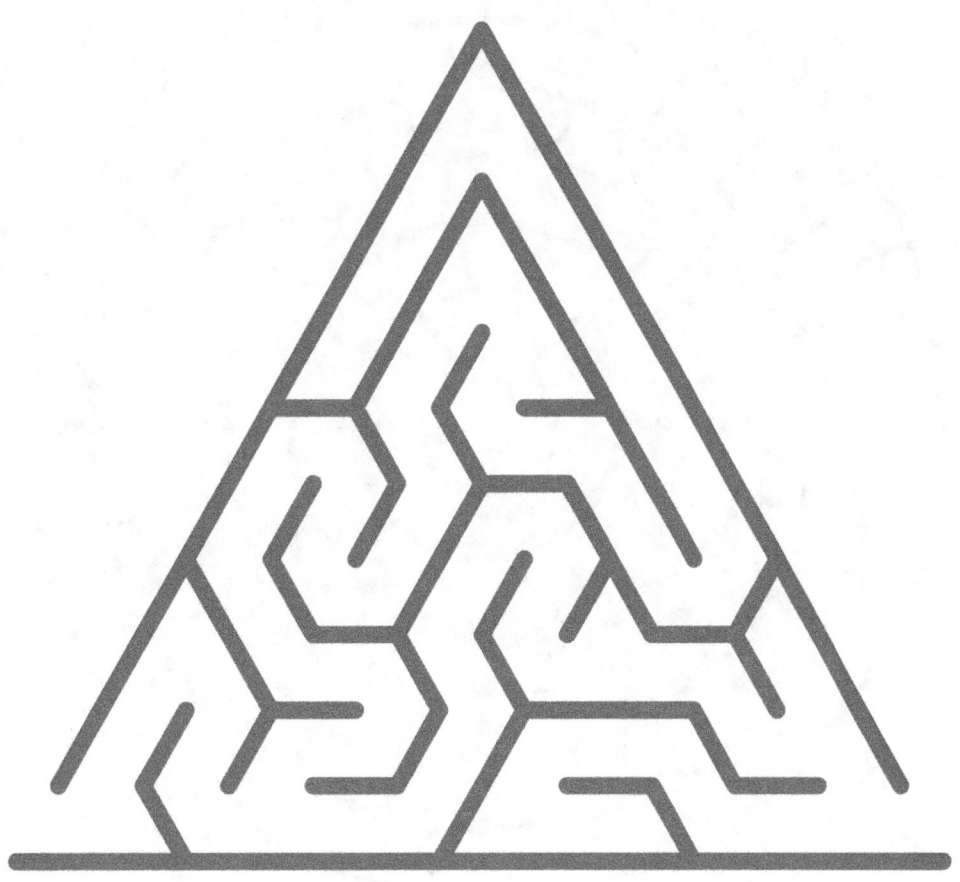

Maze 88 - Medium

Maze 89 - Simple

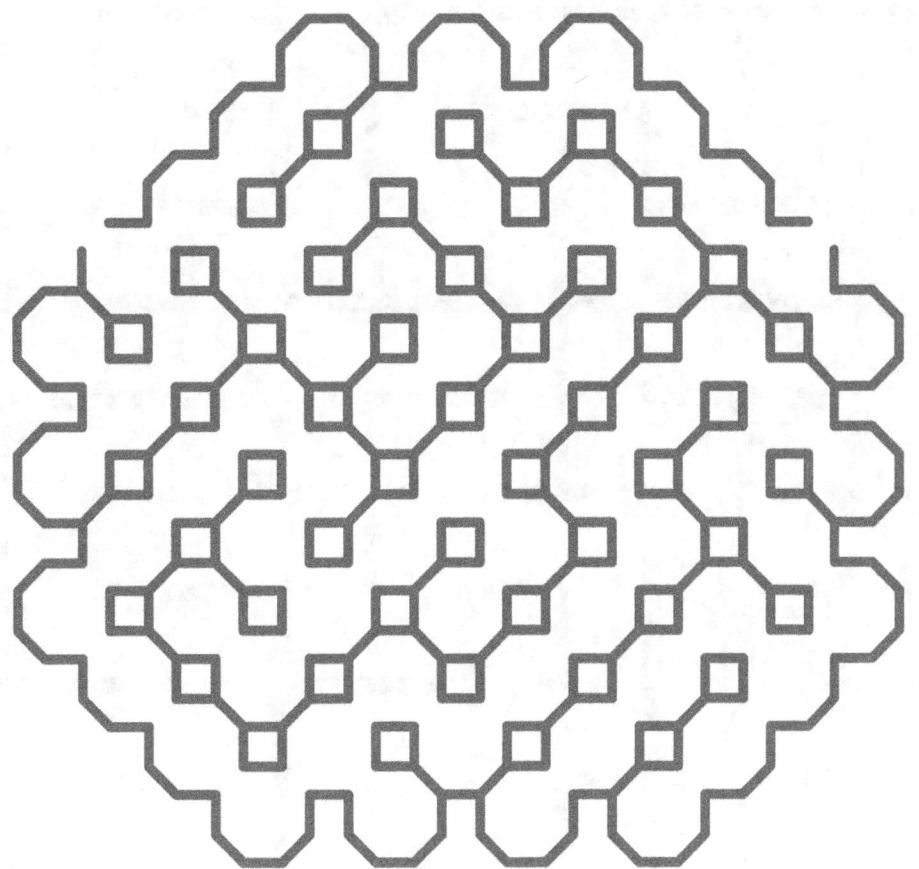

Maze 90 - Simple

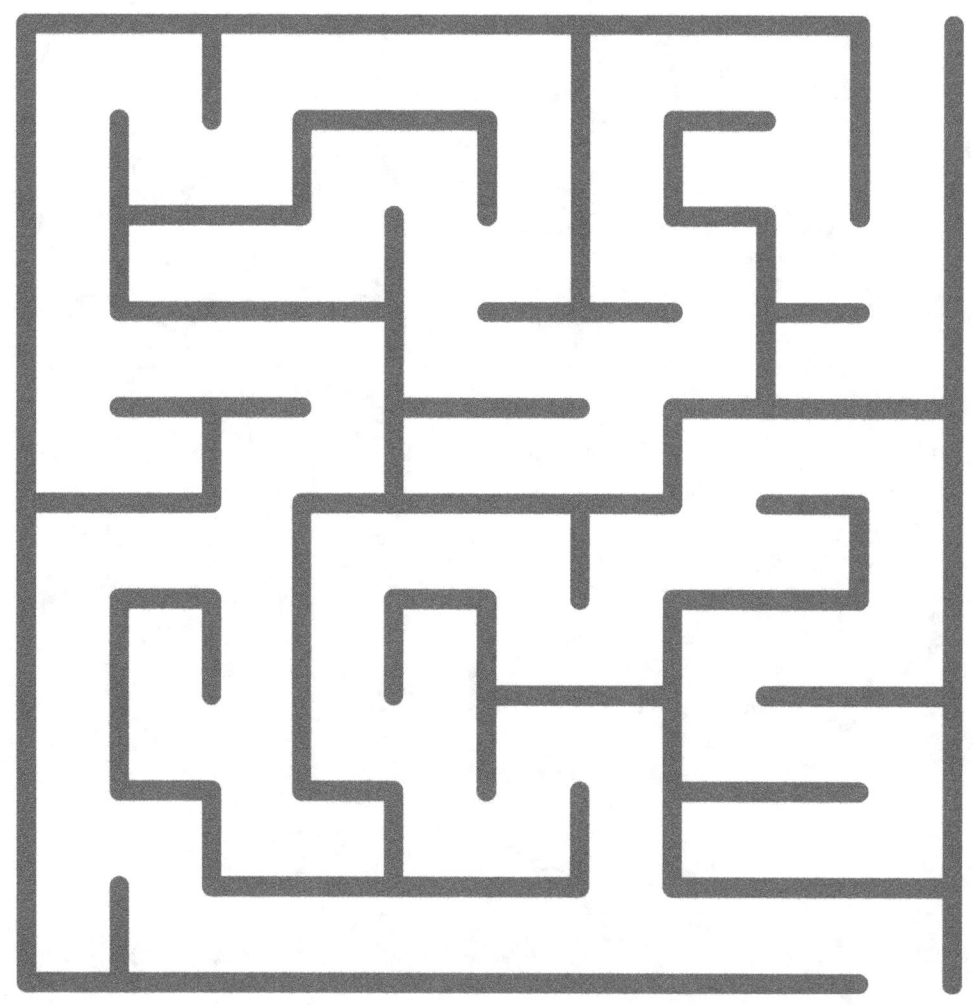

Maze 91 - Medium

Maze 92 - Simple

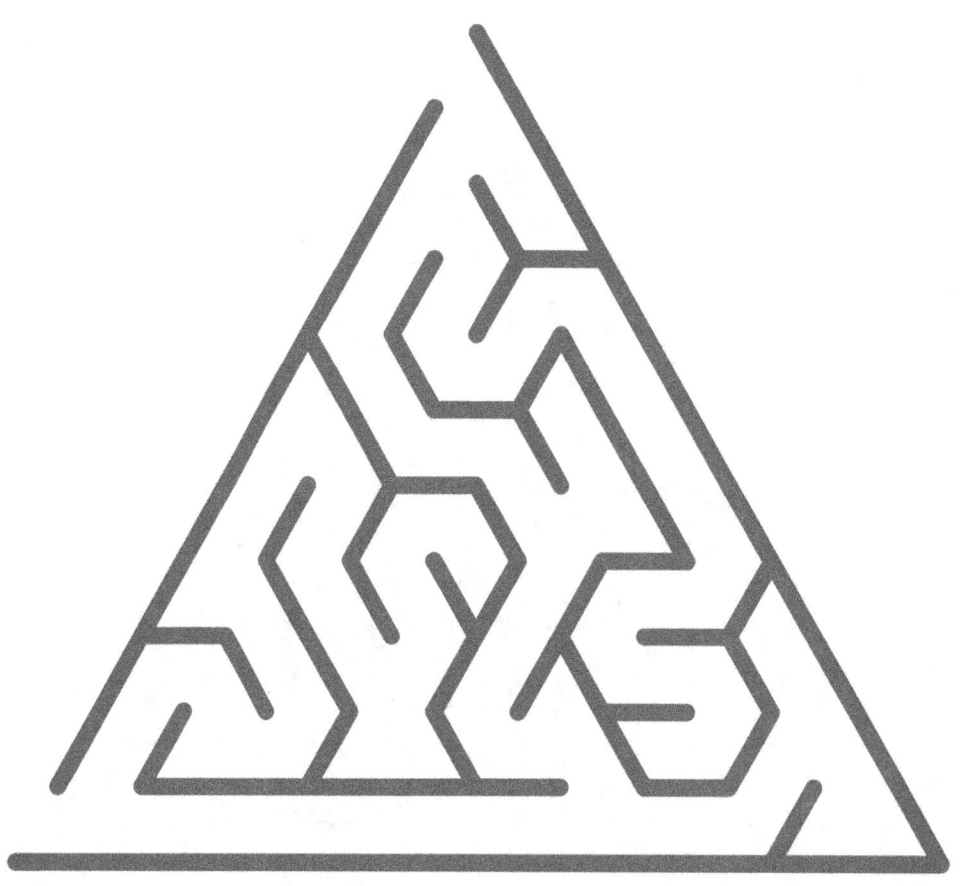

Maze 93 - Medium

Maze 94 - Medium

Maze 95 - Medium

Maze 96 - Simple

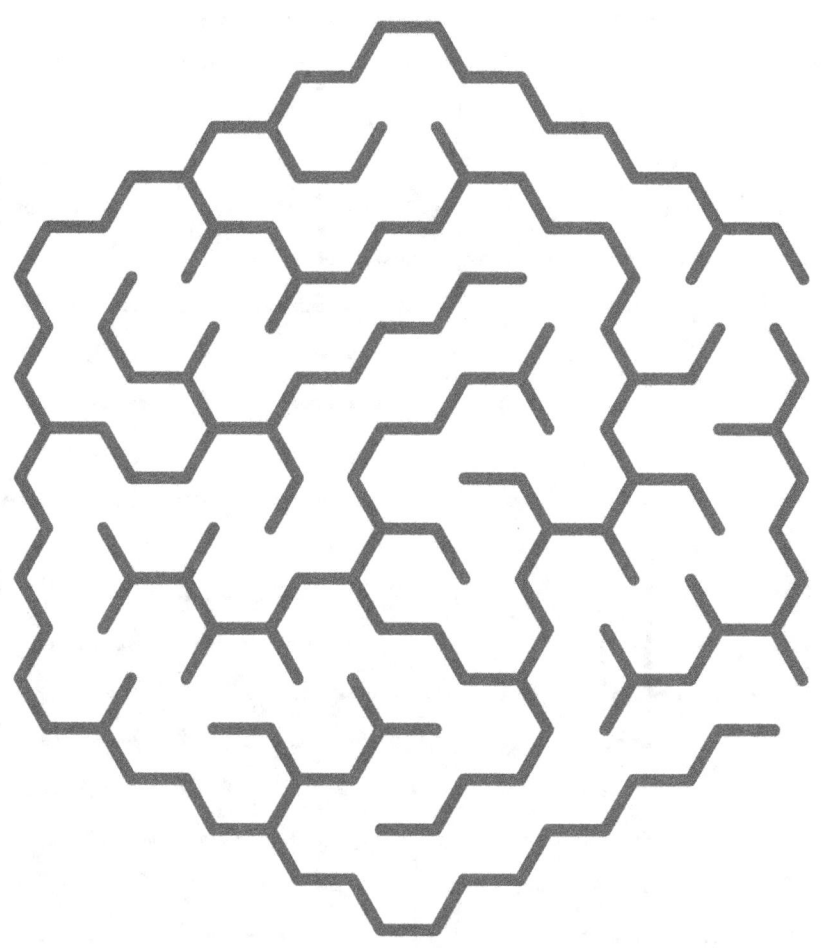

Maze 97 - Medium

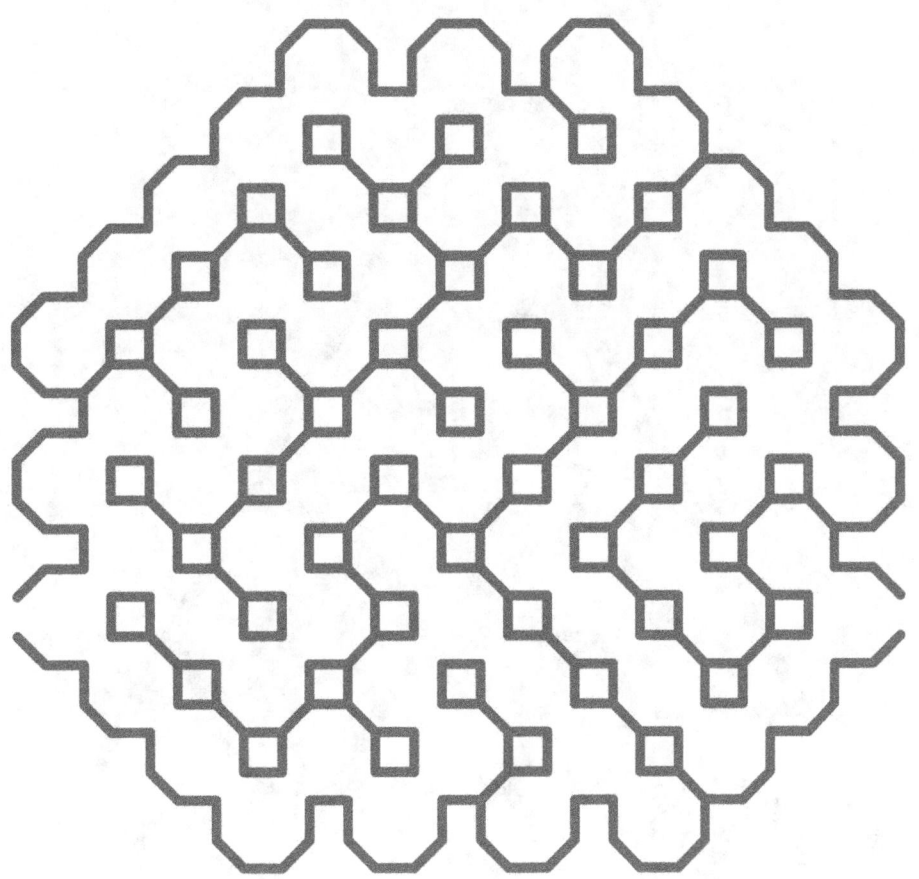

Maze 98 - Simple

Maze 99 - Medium

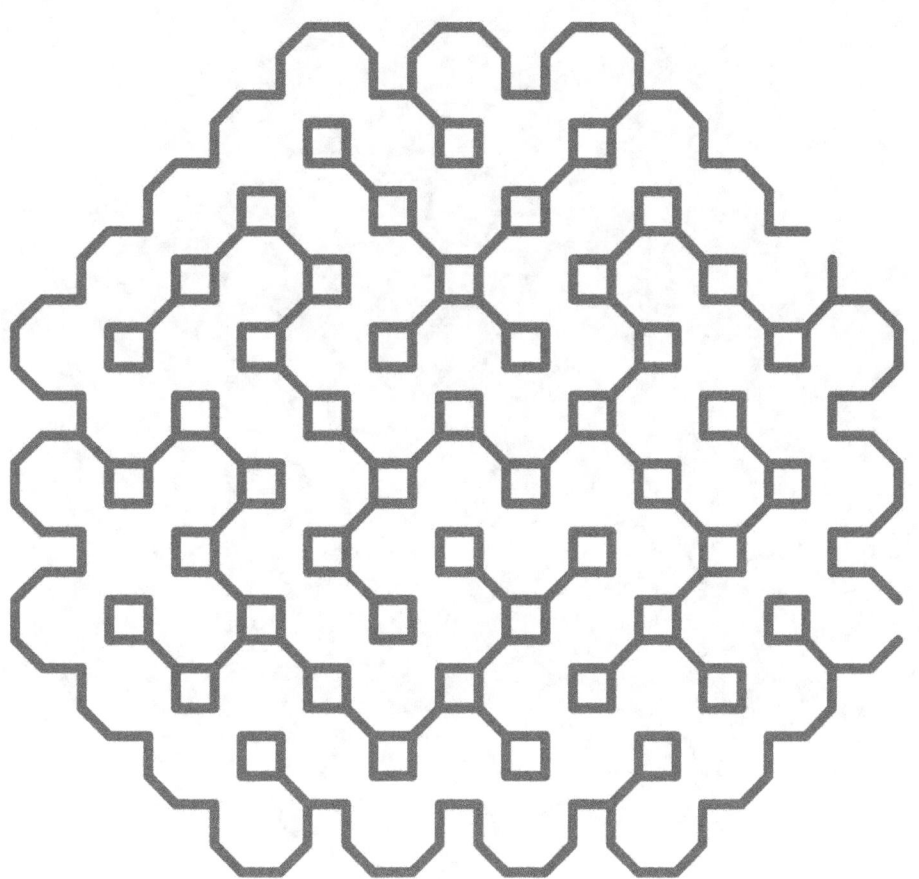

Maze 100 - Medium

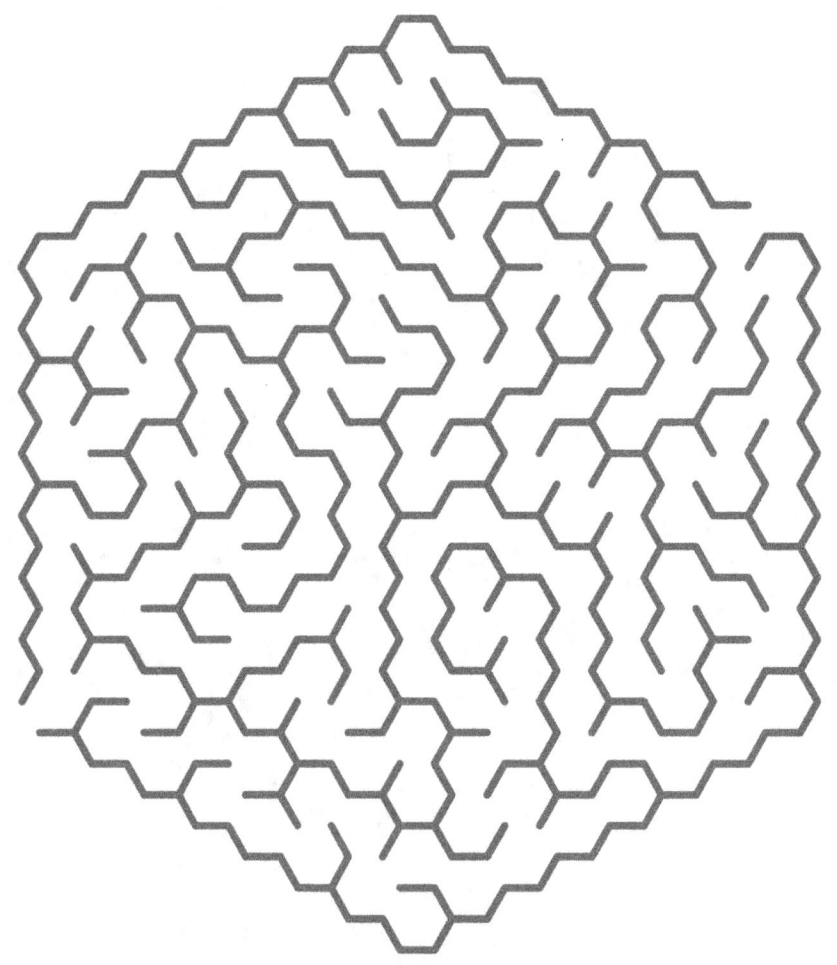

www.ingramcontent.com/pod-product-compliance
Lightning Source LLC
LaVergne TN
LVHW060207080526
838202LV00052B/4204